Maine

MAINE BY ROAD

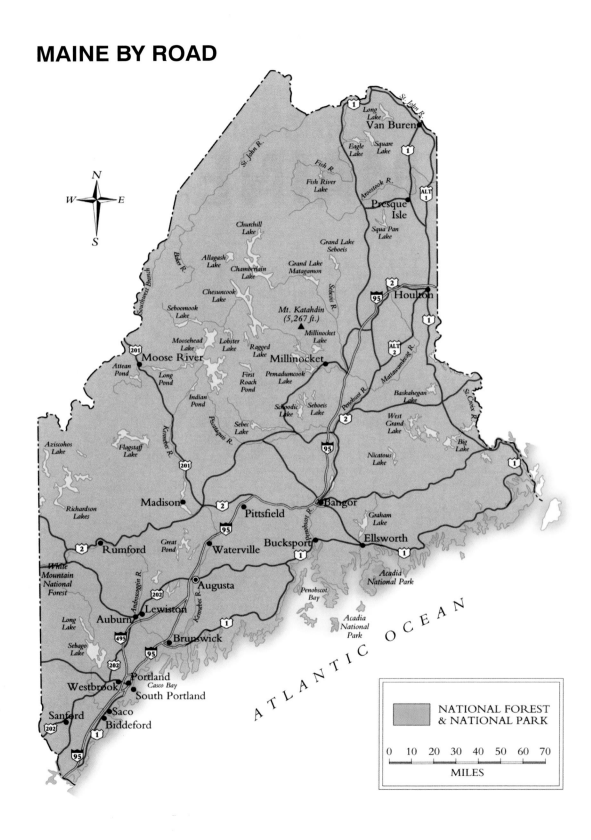

Celebrate the States

Maine

Margaret Dornfeld and Joyce Hart

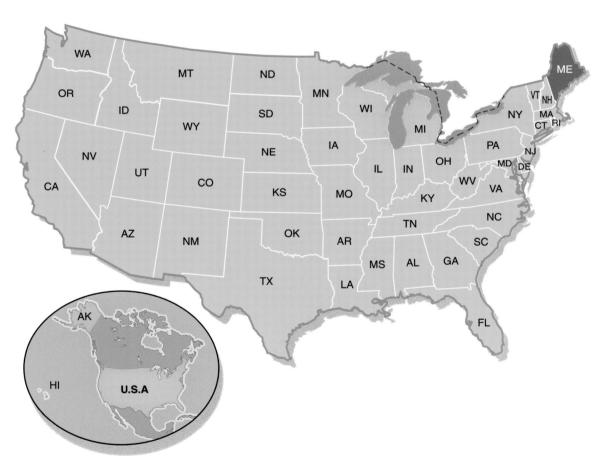

Marshall Cavendish
Benchmark
New York

Other Marshall Cavendish Offices:
Marshall Cavendish Ltd. 5th Floor, 32-38 Saffron Hill, London EC1N 8 FH, UK • Marshall Cavendish International (Asia) Private Limited, 1 New Industrial Road, Singapore 536196 • Marshall Cavendish International (Thailand) Co Ltd. 253 Asoke, 12th Flr, Sukhumvit 21 Road, Klongtoey Nua, Wattana, Bangkok 10110, Thailand • Marshall Cavendish (Malaysia) Sdn Bhd, Times Subang, Lot 46, Subang Hi-Tech Industrial Park, Batu Tiga, 40000 Shah Alam, Selangor Darul Ehsan, Malaysia

Marshall Cavendish is a trademark of Times Publishing Limited

All websites were available and accurate when this book was sent to press.

Library of Congress Cataloging-in-Publication Data
Dornfeld, Margaret.
Maine / by Margaret Dornfeld and Joyce Hart.—2nd ed.
p. cm. — (Celebrate the states)
Summary: "Provides comprehensive information on the geography, history, wildlife, governmental structure, economy, cultural diversity, peoples, religion, and landmarks of Maine"—Provided by publisher.
Includes bibliographical references and index.
ISBN 978-0-7614-4726-9
1. Maine—Juvenile literature. I. Hart, Joyce, 1954– II. Title.

F19.3.D67 2011
974.1—dc22
2009002583

Editor: Christine Florie
Co-Editor: Denise Pangia
Publisher: Michelle Bisson
Art Director: Anahid Hamparian
Series Designer: Adam Mietlowski

Photo research and layout by Marshall Cavendish International (Asia) Private Limited—
Thomas Khoo, Benson Tan and Gu Jing

Cover Photo by Photolibrary

The photographs in this book are used by permission and through the courtesy of; *alt. TYPE/REUTERS*: 72; *Corbis*: 17, 23, 43, 45, 123, 132, 137; *Getty Images*: 60, 71, 88, 117, 119, 121, 122, 124, 126, 127, 128, 129, 131; *Photolibrary*: back cover, 8, 11, 16, 19, 20, 21, 28, 29, 30, 33, 35, 39, 41, 55, 58, 76, 78, 81, 90, 95, 101, 106, 109, 112; *Photolibrary/Alamy*: 26, 48, 51, 64, 66, 68, 75, 84, 86, 92, 98, 100, 102, 109, 116, 118, 120, 125, 133, 134, 135.

Printed in Malaysia
1 3 5 6 4 2

Contents

Maine Is . . .

Maine is a place of many different vistas . . .

"It is a country full of evergreen trees, of mossy silver birches and watery maples, the ground dotted with insipid, small red berries, and strewn with damp and moss-grown rocks, . . . the forest resounding at rare intervals with a note of the chickadee, the blue-jay, and the woodpecker, the scream of the fish-hawk and the eagle, the laugh of the loon, and the whistle of ducks along the solitary streams."
—writer Henry David Thoreau

"I made a garden on the top of the rocky isle of Monhegan in May that grew so well that it served for sallets [salads] in June and July."
—explorer Captain John Smith

"Two or three miles up the river, one beautiful country."
—a Maine Indian, describing the Penobscot River valley to Thoreau

"I looked along the San Juan Islands and the coast of California, but I couldn't find the palette of green, granite, and dark blue that you can only find in Maine."
—actor Parker Stevenson

. . . and a place that makes people grow resilient.

"Maine's long and cold winters may help keep our state's population low, but our harsh climate also accounts for what is unique and valuable about our land and our people."
—former U.S. Democratic representative from Maine Tom Allen

"What happens to me when I cross the Piscataqua and plunge rapidly into Maine at a cost of seventy-five cents in toll? I cannot describe it. I do not ordinarily spy a partridge in a pear tree, or three French hens, but I do have the sensation of having received a gift from a true love."

—writer E. B. White

Maine keeps a strong hold on the people who call it home.

"There was a fascination to it: flies and blackflies and mosquitoes. . . . You never shaved and never washed. Why, it was a hell of a place, but nevertheless you couldn't help but like it."

—retired lumberman Frank Dowling

"All I know is that history repeats itself and people are going to want to experience the world. But I know then they are going to have a better appreciation for what is here in Maine."

—governor of Maine John Baldacci

Mention Maine to some people, and they react as if it were a land far away, as unfamiliar a place as a country on the other side of the world. To those who know the wild interior landscape, the scenic charm of the rocky coastline, and the fortitude it requires to make it through the state's bitterly cold winters, Maine is the only place they want to call home. While summer tourists clamor for the quaint atmosphere that only cities like Bar Harbor can offer, Maine's fishers work diligently in the high northern seas. While winter tourists glide down the tall, snow-crested mountainsides, Mainers plow their driveways and stoke the fires to keep their homes warm. There are many different faces of this farthest northeastern New England state, and Mainers know them all very well.

Chapter One

One Beautiful Country

Maine forms the easternmost part of the region known as New England, far up in the northeastern corner of the United States. Its upper half is surrounded by Canada, with New Brunswick to the northeast and Quebec to the northwest. Its long southeastern edge lies along the Atlantic Ocean with a rocky shore. New Hampshire, the only state that borders Maine, lies to the southwest.

Maine's rugged terrain emerged more than 500 million years ago, when molten rock bubbling up from deep inside the earth pushed toward the surface to form rows of mountains all over northern New England. About 25,000 years ago a huge glacier spread down from Canada and smothered the land. Over a period of thousands of years the movement of this thick sheet of ice flattened the tops of Maine's highest peaks and gouged out its riverbeds. Sand and clay dragged by the ice formed ridges along its highlands. When the glacier withdrew, somewhere between 18,000 and 11,000 years ago, the ocean rose higher than it ever had before. Today's Maine coast emerged during this dramatic moment in the

Baxter State Park contains forty-six mountain peaks and ridges, eighteen of which exceed an elevation of 3,000 feet. Baxter Peak (shown on the left) is the highest in the park at 5,267 feet.

land's history. Its rocky bluffs and rugged islands are actually mountains whose valleys have been flooded by the sea.

Maine can be divided into regions that nearly cut the state into three equal parts: the Coastal Lowlands, which follow the shoreline; the Eastern New England Upland, which runs up the middle of the state; and the White Mountains, which make up the western boundaries.

THE LONG ROCKY SHORE OF THE COASTAL LOWLANDS

Dazzling and desolate, savage as well as serene, the state's seacoast is Maine at its most dramatic. Maine's shoreline is long and winding. Measured as the crow flies from Canada to the New Hampshire border, it covers a distance of about 250 miles. But if you considered all the twists and turns of its bays, inlets, capes, and peninsulas and pulled them straight, the coastline would stretch for almost 3,500 miles—that's as far as the distance from Maine to Florida.

One of the most distinctive features of the Maine coast is the way its stony points and secluded coves crowd together so that the next glimpse of sparkling water never seems far away. Maine resident Harriet Beecher Stowe wrote that as you travel along the shore, "The sea, living, beautiful and life-giving, seems . . . to be everywhere about you behind, before, around. . . . Now, you catch a peep of it on your right hand, among tufts of oak and maple, and anon it spreads on your left to a majestic sheet of silver, among rocky shores, hung with dark pines, hemlocks, and spruces."

More than five thousand islands dot the Maine seacoast. Some are large enough for hundreds of people to live on; others are too small to support a single tree. About two-thirds of the way up the coast looms the most spectacular of these, called Mount Desert Island (pronounced

De-SERT). This beautiful island is the main site of Acadia National Park, the first national park east of the Mississippi River. Waves crash against pink granite cliffs along the rim of this densely forested cluster of offshore mountains. Its highest point, Cadillac Mountain, towers 1,530 feet above sea level. The coast to the north of Mount Desert Island is especially wild and lonely. Its rocky shore zigzags all the way out to West Quoddy Head, the most easterly point in the United States.

Mount Desert Island, the home of Acadia National Park, was formed by a mile-high glacier millions of years ago.

It is on the southern coast of Maine that you meet most of the people who live in this state, which, according to a 2008 estimate, is 1,316,456. It is here that Maine's largest city, Portland, sits on the breathtaking Casco Bay, about 50 miles north of the New Hampshire border. Other cities you will find on the Coastal Lowlands include Brunswick, Belfast, Bucksport, Bangor, and Bar Harbor. Farther east the rocky coast gives way to a mixture of historic seaports, marshland, and sandy beaches.

Long before the first tourists came to the area, Maine's plentiful fish and lumber attracted ships from around the world. To New England ship captains Maine was just a quick sail down east—meaning east and downwind (with the wind at their backs)—of Boston. Today, "Down East" is as much a cultural nickname as it is a geographical one. It's a term some people use to mean the whole state of Maine and everything that goes along with it. But to most Mainers the real Down East is the coast—and the farther north and east you go, the more you get that combination of rawness, solitude, and simplicity that gives Maine its distinctive flavor.

FARMLANDS IN THE NEW ENGLAND UPLANDS

Just inland from the coast and curving north along the New Brunswick border, the land rises into an area of rolling hills, ridges, and river valleys known as the New England Uplands. Thousands of lakes and ponds adorn this countryside. It once was covered by forests, but people have cleared much of the land to make room for crops and livestock.

A checkerboard of woodlands and open fields, the Uplands are home to most of Maine's farms and mill towns. Apple orchards and dairy farms can be found toward the south and around the capital, Augusta.

LAND AND WATER

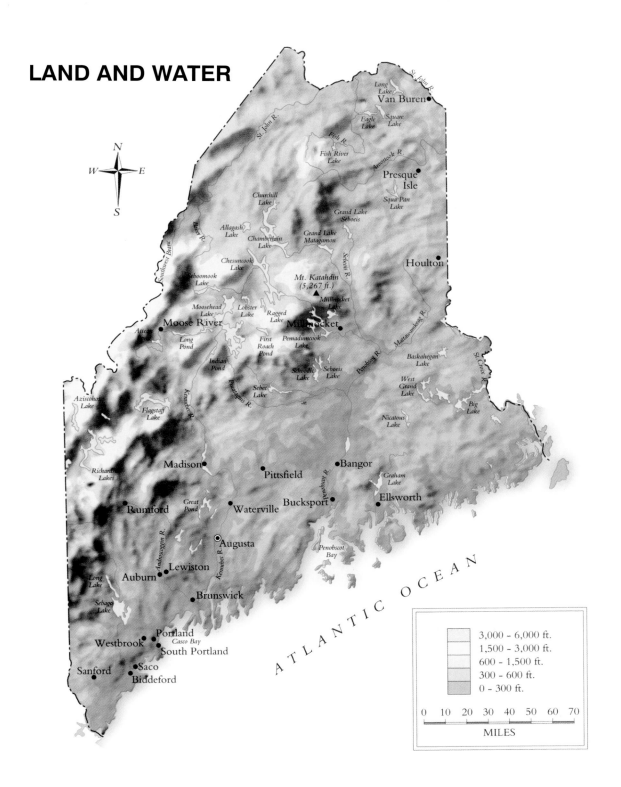

N
W · E
S

Van Buren

St. John R.
Long Lake
Square Lake
Eagle Lake
Fish R.
Fish River Lake

Aroostook R.

Presque Isle

Squa Pan Lake

St. John R.

Churchill Lake

Grand Lake Seboeis

Houlton

Allagash Lake
Chamberlain Lake

Grand Lake Matagamon

Seboeis R.

River R.

Chesuncook Lake

Seboomook Lake

Mt. Katahdin (5,267 ft.)

Millinocket Lake

Mattawamkeag R.

Southwest Branch

Moosehead Lake
Lobster Lake
Ragged Lake

Millinocket

Baskahegan Lake

Moose River

Long Pond

First Roach Pond

Pemadumcook Lake

Penobscot R.

West Grand Lake

St. Croix R.

Indian Pond

Schoodic Lake
Seboeis Lake

Sebec Lake

Kennebec R.

Piscataquis R.

Nicatous Lake

Big Lake

Aziscohos Lake

Flagstaff Lake

Madison

Pittsfield

Bangor

Graham Lake

Ellsworth

Richardson Lakes

Rumford

Great Pond

Waterville

Bucksport

Androscoggin R.

Augusta

Penobscot Bay

Long Lake

Auburn
Lewiston

Kennebec R.

Brunswick

Sebago Lake

Portland
Westbrook
Casco Bay
South Portland

Sanford
Saco
Biddeford

ATLANTIC OCEAN

	3,000 – 6,000 ft.
	1,500 – 3,000 ft.
	600 – 1,500 ft.
	300 – 600 ft.
	0 – 300 ft.

0 10 20 30 40 50 60 70

MILES

THE OLD SOW WHIRLPOOL

Claimed to be the second-largest tidal whirlpool in the world and the largest in the Western Hemisphere, the Old Sow Whirlpool reaches 250 feet in diameter. It can be seen off Moose Island not far from Eastport, Maine. The whirling motions and the sucking sounds they cause, which may be the reason for the name, are due to the extreme tides in this area and the makeup of the floor of the bays.

The bay areas along the Maine coast are said to be flooded. This means that what was once dry land was flooded as the ocean level rose when the Ice Age came to an end. So the floors of the bays are made up of the bases of mountains, which create currents as the water flows around them. Added to this are the tides, which can vary 16 feet or more between high and low tides. As the water rushes in during a high tide, the currents swirl against each other and often create whirlpools, which are powerful, circular currents of water. The Old Sow Whirlpool is not known to be particularly dangerous to motorized boats, and rides through it are offered to tourists. However, people on sailboats are warned to avoid these waters during the onrush of high tide.

Farther north, near the coast, stretch the blueberry barrens, where one of Maine's leading crops is grown. But the largest farms sit at the top of the state, in remote Aroostook County. The Aroostook highlands are the remains of a slowly eroding plateau. Here the broad fields between the towns of Presque Isle, Caribou, and Fort Fairfield make up the heart of Maine's potato-growing region. In June and July potato blossoms blanket the land like a dusting of delicate pink snow.

BEAUTY OF THE WHITE MOUNTAINS

The farthest western region of Maine is mostly made up of the White Mountains, a part of the Appalachian Range, which runs down the East Coast of the United States, beginning in Maine and ending in northern Georgia. It is in this area that residents and visitors realize why Maine is called the Pine Tree State. In fact, northern Maine is part of the Great North Woods, which stretches from Maine to Minnesota. In this region of Maine forests cover just about every square inch of land, spreading like a blue-green carpet.

The Longfellow Mountains form the backbone of the Great North Woods. Near the heart of the state rises the mile-high Mount Katahdin. American Indians once told legends of a spirit that guarded Maine's highest peak, but that doesn't keep visitors from climbing it today. "The experience is just too much," says hiker Jeff Wood of Augusta. "As soon as you start past the tree line, the hustle and bustle world just seems to slip away. The quiet is overwhelming as the wind passes along the top; it's just you and the mountain." Katahdin's summit marks one end of the Appalachian Trail, a 2,064-mile hiking path that winds through the mountains of the eastern United States.

Looking down from Katahdin, you can see Maine's largest lakes: Moosehead, Chesuncook, and Millinocket. Farther southwest lie the smaller Flagstaff Lake and the Rangeley Lakes. These stunning bodies of water feed the Kennebec, Penobscot, and Androscoggin rivers, which tumble southeast and spill into the Atlantic Ocean. Northwest of Katahdin are a series of long, narrow lakes known as the Allagash Wilderness Waterway. These flow north into the wild Allagash River and finally the Saint John River, which marks Maine's northern border before veering off into New Brunswick.

Mount Katahdin, the centerpiece of Baxter State Park, is the highest mountain in Maine.

Situated in the Longfellow Mountains in Maine's Highland Region, Moosehead Lake is the source of the Kennebec River.

Maine's woods are also threaded with thousands of smaller rivers, streams, and marshes. "I traveled constantly with the impression that I was in a swamp," commented the writer Henry David Thoreau, who explored the Maine woods in the nineteenth century. Fed by up to 80 inches of precipitation every year, these forest wetlands make the woods a paradise for all kinds of living things.

SAVING MOUNT KATAHDIN

Maine owes its largest and most majestic state park to the remarkable generosity of just one man: Percival P. Baxter. Born in 1876 in Portland to a wealthy family devoted to politics, Baxter became governor of Maine in 1921. When it came to saving Maine's wild lands, Baxter was anything but tight-fisted. First as a state legislator and then as governor, he kept trying to keep Mount Katahdin beautiful by making it into a state park. Baxter never succeeded, so when he left office he decided to save Katahdin a different way—by buying it himself. In 1930 he purchased 6,000 acres from the Great Northern Paper Company, then donated them to the state the next year. Little by little over the next thirty years, he bought and passed on to the people of Maine a total of 202,000 acres. That land makes up Baxter State Park today.

When Baxter died in 1969, he knew he was leaving something wonderful behind. He once wrote:

Man is born to die, his works are short lived.
Buildings crumble, monuments decay, wealth vanishes.
But Katahdin in all its glory,
Forever shall remain the Mountain of the People of Maine.

PLANTS AND ANIMALS

A rich variety of plants thrives in Maine's cool, damp climate. Of these none are more striking than the dark evergreens and beautiful hardwoods that make up its forests. Almost 90 percent of Maine is covered with trees.

Dark stands of spruce and fir take root in the thin, rocky soil of the mountains, riverbanks, and coastline. These woods merge with cedar and tamarack in low, swampy areas and with hemlock along hillsides. In places where the soil has lots of sand or clay in it, the state tree, the eastern white pine, prevails. Trees that lose their leaves, like beech, birch, and maple, often mingle with the evergreens, and where older forests have been cleared, these leafy trees dominate the land.

Maine's older evergreen forests are dense, mossy, and encrusted with lichens of all kinds. A typical lichen is usnea, or old-man's beard, which trails in wisps from the boughs of spruce trees. In the spring fragile wildflowers such as the trout lily, trillium, violet, and pink lady's slipper nestle on the floor of leafy woodlands. Nearby marshes are thick with water-loving plants such as bog rosemary, leatherleaf, skunk cabbage, and Labrador tea.

A star attraction of Maine's woods is the state animal, the moose. Standing 6 to 7 feet tall at the shoulder and weighing up to 1,200 pounds,

Maine designated the moose its official state animal in 1979.

this lumbering giant, with its long, spindly legs and thickset body, seems built for wading in marshes and trudging across deep winter snows. Moose can show up pretty much anywhere in the Pine Tree State, but you're most likely to spot one in the north, along the edge of a lake, marsh, or slow-moving river. They love to snack on water plants and the tender green leaves of saplings.

Besides moose, all kinds of smaller mammals take refuge in Maine's evergreen forests, including red squirrels, chipmunks, and pine martens. Another north woods animal, the spruce grouse, can be hard to detect but is so tame that if you come across one, it may even let you stroke its feathers. Also known as a fool hen, the spruce grouse would have been wiped out long ago if it tasted better. Most animals find it indigestible, however, because it eats so many spruce and fir needles.

The spruce grouse makes its home in the coniferous forests of Maine.

Woodland animals such as the white-tailed deer, beaver, snowshoe hare, red fox, bobcat, mink, and porcupine can be found all over the state, from the mountains to the coast. Black bears like to feast on the mountain cranberries and blueberries that grow in clearings. Canada lynx are also found in the northern part of the state. Wildlife thrives on the coast as well. Sea urchins, mussels, starfish, and periwinkles cluster in tide pools—pockets of seawater trapped by the rocks when the tide goes out. Harbor seals cruise in and out of quiet inlets as ospreys and bald eagles soar over the water from the tops of pines.

PROJECT PUFFIN

One of Maine's most unusual seabirds is getting a lift these days, thanks to a conservation effort known as Project Puffin. Once a common sight Down East, Atlantic puffins were nearly eliminated from the state in the late nineteenth century, when a craze for puffin feathers—used to decorate ladies' hats—made them a prime target for hunters. Puffins became a protected species in the early 1900s, but they never regained anything close to their former numbers. In 1973 just two fragile puffin colonies remained in Maine, on Matinicus Rock and Machias Seal Island.

Adult puffins, which are no more than 13 inches long, dive from the air or the surface of the sea to catch fish. They swallow fish while still underwater, unless they are bringing the catch home for their young. Puffins usually return to the place where they were raised to mate and start their own families. So a group of biologists with the National Audubon Society took some puffin chicks from breeding grounds in Canada and brought them to Eastern Egg Rock, the former site of a puffin colony. They kept the babies alive by giving them vitamin-fortified fish each day. Between 1973 and 1986 more than nine hundred puffins were introduced to Eastern Egg Rock this way. Biologists then repeated the project at Seal Island National Wildlife Refuge. As of 2009 the puffins were continuing to thrive.

Down East winters are typically long and bitter. January temperatures average 20 degrees Fahrenheit in Portland and as low as 8 °F in the far north. Lakes and rivers freeze over, ice creeps into the harbors, and deep snows blanket the western mountains. Winter begins in November and can last as long as six months. Most Mainers look forward to the "ice-out"— that moment when the ice on the rivers cracks, separates, and starts drifting out to sea in giant hunks.

When spring arrives, streams and rivers all over the state swell into a torrent of melted ice and snow. Not so long ago it was on these surging waterways that Maine's lumbermen risked life and limb driving logs from deep in the woods toward sawmills near Bangor, Machias, and Lewiston downstream. The thaw only lasts a couple of weeks. By the end of May violet-blue, pink, and white lupines carpet the roadsides along the coast, and the gentle, breezy days of summer have begun.

People flock to Maine from all around to bask in perfect summers. The only real drawback to this time of year is the bugs: in June and July the woods are abuzz with gnats, blackflies, and mosquitoes. Out in the open, though, mild, mostly sunny days and cool nights keep the state comfortable all season long. In Portland daytime temperatures hover around 70 °F, dropping at night to 50 °F. Sometimes a thick fog will roll in and settle over the coast, cloaking the islands in a veil of mystery.

As August turns to September, autumn sets the Maine woods ablaze in magnificent shades of red, gold, and amber. Fall is also the peak time for hurricanes, which can slam the coast with winds as high as 90 miles per hour. For instance, back in 1985, Hurricane Gloria hit the coastline with winds of 86 miles per hour. Then in 1991 Hurricane Bob brought

From the last week of September to the third week of October, trees show off their red, gold, and amber hues, making Maine the top destination for viewing fall foliage.

slightly lesser winds, at 61 miles per hour, but it dumped almost 8 inches of rain on Portland and caused $26 million in damage. But when the weather is calm, the cool, crisp days and brilliant foliage can make autumn Maine's loveliest time of the year.

PROTECTING THE LAND

Maine has fewer people per square mile than any other state east of the Mississippi. Nearly half of its population lives along the coast, leaving huge areas in the west and north sparsely populated. Maine's northernmost and poorest unincorporated territories include 10.5 million acres of woodlands—more than half the state's total.

Yet even in the forests people have left their mark. The 250-foot-tall pines that towered over the land when Europeans first arrived have long since disappeared—loggers cut them down and sold the wood to shipbuilders back in the nineteenth century. Lumbering, one of the state's biggest industries, still shapes the landscape. In some parts of the forest Maine loggers use a method known as clear-cutting, where they harvest all the trees in one area at once. This is usually the cheapest way to cut timber, and in the 1970s and 1980s it was used widely. As a result, many large sections of Maine's woods are dotted with just the stumps of the trees that used to grow there.

People have also transformed the state's rivers. About 125 dams control Maine's waterways. Although they help fuel the economy by providing hydroelectric power, they can also lower water quality and block the path of migratory fish—fish that are born in the river, swim out to sea, and then return to their birthplace, or spawning grounds, to lay eggs for the next generation. For example, more than ten species of migratory fish once spawned in the Kennebec River, but their numbers have dwindled because of dams.

To help get the Kennebec fish population back up again, state and federal authorities made a bold move. Instead of renovating the 162-year-old Edwards Dam, near Augusta, they simply got rid of it, taking it apart in 1999. Now at least four Kennebec fish species—striped bass, Atlantic salmon, American shad, and short-nosed sturgeon—can reach their spawning grounds 17 miles upriver from the old dam site. Alewives, a migrating herring that must pass dams upstream, are also beginning to return. Biologists look forward to the day when other species that once spawned at the top of the Kennebec return to the river as well.

A similar project is occurring on the Penobscot River. Through the collaboration of the hydropower company PPL Corporation, the Penobscot Indian Nation, seven conservation groups, and state and federal agencies, the river is going to be restored so that eleven important species of sea-run fish can return to their ancient spawning grounds upriver. In August 2008 plans were announced for the removal of two dams, the Veazie and the Great Works, and for the construction of a fishway on the Howland Dam to allow easier access upriver. This will open hundreds of miles of river habitat to salmon and other fish.

These innovations and modifications to the landscape are helping to keep Maine a beautiful state that supports the plants, wildlife, and people who live there.

Chapter Two

Maine, Past to Present

The past is alive in the Pine Tree State. Maine's American-Indian heritage lives on in the names of its rivers, lakes, and mountains. The state's beautiful harbors, quiet coves, and broad inlets whisper of an age when tall-masted ships brought precious cargo from halfway around the world. Even the forests that once sheltered hardworking men and women hold stories from the past that are waiting to be told.

THE FIRST PEOPLE

Historians believe the first people to live in what is present-day Maine arrived almost 11,500 years ago. Not much is known about these early residents, referred to by scientists as Paleo-Indians. It is likely, though, that they used stone tools and hunted caribou, an animal related to the reindeer that once roamed the land in enormous herds. Fluted points used on spears and other artifacts left by these people have been found in Maine.

From about 3,500 to 8,000 years ago Maine was home to a group known today as the Red Paint people. They got their name from the

Maine's natural beauty and bountiful wildlife attracted early settlers to the region.

graves they left behind, which contain stones and other objects that are colored with reddish clay. Scientists believe at that time these people were skilled in swordfish hunting, which was quite a feat. Even today, with modern equipment and larger boats, the swordfish is a huge challenge to bring in. Evidence of this culture can be found at what is called the Nevin Shell Heap, located south of Blue Hill Bay on the coast. Hammerstones and other artifacts have been found in this pile of burned shells and animal bones.

Another Red Paint site is located on North Haven Island, in Penobscot Bay. An archaeological find called the Turner Site contained fish hooks and barbed spear tips.

The nomadic Paleo-Indians hunted large animals, such as caribou.

Many centuries later, somewhere around 2800 BCE, native people who made ceramic pots arrived. These people were the first to live in wigwams, which are coned-shaped structures often made of animals skins, in Maine.

Information about early people in what is now called Maine jumps to about 1400 CE. At that time there were approximately 20,000 American Indians living in the area.

A large part of the Abenaki diet was corn, which they harvested in late summer and early fall.

They were loosely related, talking similar languages and sharing similar cultures. The Abenaki (also spelled Abnaki) lived in the southwestern part of Maine. The Penobscot mainly lived in the south central portion. Along the southern coastline lived the Passamaquoddy; with the Maliseet and the Micmac residing in the northeast. Many of these early people lived in wigwams. The first agriculture in Maine was practiced by these tribal people, especially those who lived in the southwestern region. They grew corn, beans, and squash. The people who lived in the eastern region of what is now Maine were mostly hunters and gatherers of wild plants.

As more and more European trappers, adventurers, and settlers moved into the area, many of these American Indians died from the diseases that the new arrivals inadvertently passed along. As each different tribe dwindled in number, the survivors joined with one another. Many of the mixed tribes migrated into Quebec to live with larger groups, while others remained within the state of Maine.

ACADIA

Just six years after Christopher Columbus became the first European known to land in the New World, an explorer named John Cabot, who was in the service of England, arrived in North America. In 1498 he sailed up the Maine coast, planted the English flag in what is now Canada, and claimed the entire area for the English king. Cabot may have been the first European to set eyes on Maine, but no one is really sure. What is certain is that his voyage helped pave the way for the Europeans who would one day settle its shores.

In 1524 another European ship sailed into Maine's waters. Its captain was the Italian explorer Giovanni da Verrazano. He was sailing for the French, who also wanted to claim land in the New World. He landed briefly near present-day Portland. In later travels to South America, Verrazano was killed.

Many years passed before the next explorers traveled to Maine, though fishermen soon began plundering its rich sea life. Little by little word spread of the wealth to be found along the coast of Maine and eastern Canada—a region known at the time as Acadia, after a mythical wonderland described by the ancient Greeks.

In 1604 a nobleman named Pierre du Gua, Sieur de Monts, set out from France with mapmaker Samuel de Champlain to scout the Acadian coast. De Monts sailed

Italian explorer Giovanni da Verrazano sailed into Maine's waters in 1524.

up the Saint Croix River, and his men set up a village on a small island there. While the other members of the expedition built houses, planted crops, and got ready to face the frigid Maine winter, de Monts and Champlain traveled down the coast. They came to a mountainous island,

THE NORSE COIN

It's hard to say for certain when Europeans first set foot in Maine, but some people believe it happened long before the 1500s. In fact, some say non-native people landed in what is now Maine more than four hundred years before Christopher Columbus was even born. Scandinavian sagas describe the travels of the Vikings, northern Europeans who sailed the Atlantic Ocean a thousand years ago. According to one story, after the Viking explorer Leif Eriksson landed in Greenland in around 1000 CE, he sailed west and started a colony called Vinland the Good. Traces of Vinland have been discovered at a place called L'Anse aux Meadows in Newfoundland, Canada. From there the Vikings may have traveled as far south as Maine. One reason to think so is a coin, discovered in 1957, that lay buried for centuries under Naskeag Point in Brooklin. This little piece of blackened silver, about the size of a dime, didn't look like much at first. But an expert later confirmed it was minted under the reign of King Olaf Kyrre, who ruled Norway from 1067 to 1093 CE. The Norse coin is the oldest European object ever found in the United States. Did Vikings bring it? Scientists still do not know.

which Champlain named Île des Monts Déserts (island of bare mountains), and sailed up the Penobscot River as far as present-day Bangor. By the time they got back to Saint Croix Island, de Monts' men were sick with scurvy, a condition caused by a lack of vitamin C. Almost half of them died that brutal winter. The rest fled the island as soon as the ice melted, leaving Maine's first European colony in ruins.

THE FRENCH AND INDIAN WARS

The French were not the only ones interested in the land that would one day become the state of Maine. In 1607, many years before the Pilgrims landed at Plymouth Rock in present-day Massachusetts, English colonists attempted to create the first permanent settlement in Maine at the mouth of the Kennebec River. But they too were beaten by the harsh conditions and returned the next year to Britain. The English would try again, but it would take another decade or so for their first settlements to take root.

In 1614 John Smith, famed sea captain and once president of the Jamestown Colony, in what would become Virginia, sailed to Maine. He recorded his experiences in a book called *Description of New England*. The book was widely read in Britain and eventually encouraged English settlers to return to the area of present-day Maine. To further development, seven years later, in 1621, King James I of England signed a charter that gave a group of English noblemen rights to the land that is now Maine. Most of the early settlements started out as little more than depots where fishing crews stopped to dry their catch before sailing back to Europe. Later, they grew into trading centers for fish, fur, and lumber. Early English settlements like York, Saco, Kittery, Wells, Falmouth, and Scarborough all lay along the coast, south of the Penobscot River.

With England and France both laying claim to Maine, the two nations were bound to come to blows. In 1675 the fighting began in what was called King Philip's War. This conflict was named for an American-Indian leader, Metacomet, who was known to the English as King Philip. This was a deadly war that killed thousands of people and destroyed many of the English towns. Though this conflict ended in 1676, other battles were begun, spreading throughout New England. The conflicts bear names such as King William's War (1698–1697), Queen Anne's War (1702–1713), Dummer's War (1721–1725), King George's War (1744–1748), and finally the French and Indian War, from 1754 until 1763, after which most American Indians in the area of Maine were forced north into Canada.

In the late 1600s more than six hundred colonists and three thousand Indians were killed during King Philip's War.

REVOLUTION

After the French and Indian Wars Maine's towns and villages mushroomed. Frontiersmen cleared the land and planted crops in the Kennebec and Penobscot river valleys. Maine was then part of the Massachusetts Bay Colony, and in 1770, twenty-seven Maine towns gained the right to send representatives to Boston to help make the colony's laws. Maine would remain a part of Massachusetts for about another fifty years.

When American colonists launched the War for Independence, Mainers quickly answered the call to arms. In 1775 near the coastal town of Machias, Maine patriots seized a British ship called the HMS *Margaretta*, beating the British in the first naval battle of the war. Maine's population suffered badly during the struggle that followed, as British cannons battered the villages' shores. Early in the war the largest town, Falmouth, was bombarded and nearly burned to the ground. By the time the American Revolution ended, in 1783, Maine's ports lay in ruins.

THE STATE OF MAINE

As a part of the United States, Maine tried hard to rebuild its shattered sea trade. Falmouth rose from the ashes, and in 1786 it was renamed Portland. As Maine strove to recover, it got little help from the government in Boston, for the war had left Massachusetts deeply in debt. To raise money, the state sold large pieces of property in Maine to wealthy investors. In the 1790s, the Penobscot and Passamaquoddy Indians, who once owned about two-thirds of Maine, signed treaties with Massachusetts giving up all but a small corner of their land and some hunting and

On October 16, 1775, four British warships entered the Portland Harbor, and destroyed the town of Falmouth with artillery fire.

fishing rights. Though treaties were signed, they were interpreted by the European settlers in one way and by the American Indians according to their traditions. However, the state proceeded and soon sold the Indians' land at a huge profit—mainly to lumber companies, which were growing larger and wealthier every year.

These businesses suffered when the United States declared another war on Great Britain, known as the War of 1812. Once again the British invaded the Maine coast, blocking trade in all the harbors, from Eastport down to Belfast. The officers who were trying to defend the shoreline begged the state government in Boston for reinforcements, but help never came.

"THE LUMBERMAN'S ALPHABET"

This is one of the many songs that Maine lumbermen sang to pass the time in isolated lumber camps.

E is for the Echoes that through the woods ring;

F is for the Foreman, the head of the gang.

G is for the Grindstone that swiftly goes round,

And H is for the Handle so smooth and so round. *Chorus*

I is for the Iron, with which we mark pine,

And J is for Jolly Boys, all in a line.

K is for the Keen edge our axes we keep,

And L is for the Lice that over us creep. *Chorus*

M is for the Moss that we chink into our camps,

N is for the Needle which mendeth our pants,

O is for the Owls that hoot in the night,

And P is for the Pines what we always fall right. *Chorus*

Q is for the Quarrels, which we don't have round,

R is for the River, where we drive our logs down;

S is for the Sled, so stout and so strong,

And T is for the Team to draw it along. *Chorus*

U is for Use, which we put our teams to,

And V is for the Valley, which we draw our sleds through,

And W is for Woods that we leave in the spring,

And now I have sung all I'm going to sing.

That's all.

By the time the British retreated, many Maine citizens were angry with the Massachusetts government for leaving them stranded in a time of need. Some settlers had been arguing for years that Maine should become a separate state. They had complained that Boston was too far away, that the people there didn't understand Maine's problems, and that the government taxed them unfairly. Now even more people were beginning to think Maine should break free. In 1819 the question was put to a vote. The separatists won by a landslide, and with approval from the U.S. Congress, on March 15, 1820, Maine became the twenty-third state of the Union.

POPULATION GROWTH: 1800–2000

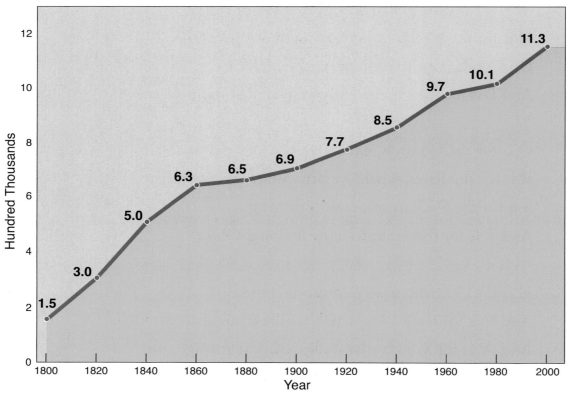

MAINE COMES OF AGE

Soon after it gained independence, Maine's economy boomed. In a few short decades the Maine coast became one of the nation's most important centers for fishing, shipping, and shipbuilding, and Bangor emerged as the lumber capital of the world. Foreign ships glided in and out of Maine's harbors, and railroads were built, ready to carry passengers from Boston to Portland and farther north. Textile and paper mills sprang up, powered by the state's swift rivers. Immigrants came by the shipload to work in the new factories or in rock quarries, cutting granite and limestone.

One of the oldest industries in Maine is shipbuilding.

Companies made fortunes harvesting ice from the Kennebec, Penobscot, and Sheepscot rivers and shipping it in huge blocks, packed with sawdust, to the far corners of the globe. Maine's ports bustled, its towns prospered, and its forests thundered with the sound of falling timber.

In some ways the nineteenth century was a golden age for the Pine Tree State, but the times weren't always peaceful. One problem was that Britain and the United States had never clearly defined Maine's northern border. Both countries claimed the land in the Aroostook territory near Madawaska in present-day Canada, an area full of valuable timber. By 1839 the border dispute had become so tense that both sides expected war. Maine prepared to send soldiers to the region and built two military outposts, Fort Fairfield and Fort Kent. But the Aroostook War ended before it even began. In 1842 U.S. secretary of state Daniel Webster and Lord Ashburton, representing the British government, settled the two countries' differences. The Webster-Ashburton Treaty solved the problem without bloodshed and determined Maine's borders for good.

While Maine was defending its claims in the north, thousands of citizens to the south and east were gearing up for another battle. People believed they were facing a much more dangerous enemy than the British. Their foe was alcohol. The world's first antialcohol organization, the Total Abstinence Society, was founded in Portland in 1815. By the 1830s similar societies had formed all over the state. The cause, known as the temperance movement, caught on quickly, and in 1851 its supporters persuaded lawmakers to ban the manufacture and sale of liquor in Maine. Though many people objected, this Maine law lasted more than eighty years.

One person who defended the Maine law was Brunswick resident Harriet Beecher Stowe. Stowe was a passionate supporter of many social causes. Before moving to Maine, she had lived in Cincinnati, Ohio, a stop on the Underground Railroad, the system of secret escape routes that brought fugitive slaves from the South to freedom in the North. Stowe was outraged by the suffering she learned about from escaped slaves, and after moving to Brunswick, she resolved to write a book showing that slavery was wrong. In 1851 she published *Uncle Tom's Cabin*, the story of a gentle slave who suffers under the hands of a cruel master. Stowe's novel took the world by storm. Between 3 and 4 million copies were sold in the United States alone, and the book was translated into forty languages.

Harriet Beecher Stowe, a Brunswick resident and author of Uncle Tom's Cabin, *supported the ban on manufacturing and selling liquor in Maine in the mid–1800s.*

Uncle Tom's Cabin heated up the debate that was already dividing the nation. Slave owners in the South insisted the region's economy depended on slavery; antislavery activists in the North wanted the practice outlawed. In 1861 tensions between the Northern and Southern states reached the boiling point, plunging the country into the Civil War. When President Abraham Lincoln called up troops, more than 70,000 Mainers marched south to fight for the Union cause. Maine gave the North thirty-one generals. One of the best known,

Joshua Lawrence Chamberlain, a professor at Bowdoin College in Brunswick, commanded Union troops as a colonel at the Battle of Gettysburg and ended his military career as general at Appomattox Court House, where the Confederacy surrendered in 1865. Chamberlain later became governor of Maine and president of Bowdoin College.

VACATIONLAND

After the Civil War Maine's economy took a downturn. The development of steel ships reduced the demand for Maine's wooden clippers, electricity threatened the ice industry, and concrete began to replace granite as the country's strongest building material. But very soon a new industry emerged to take the place of these old ones. Maine tapped into another gold mine—tourism.

Between 1870 and 1890 the sleepy village of Bar Harbor turned into a crowded resort where Bostonians, Philadelphians, and New Yorkers gathered for fresh air, sports, and summer relaxation. "A person who had not visited Bar Harbor for fifteen years would have to turn often to the mountains, the sea, and the islands to convince himself that he was really standing on the site of the puny village of that day," observed a Boston traveler in 1891. At Bar Harbor and other seaside communities wealthy vacationers built lavish summer homes. They were actually the size of mansions, though they called them cottages. Enchanted by the beauty of the island-studded coast, vacationers came every summer by steamer and train, whiled away the season yachting, playing tennis, and attending garden parties, then left again when the weather turned cool.

City dwellers eager to get a taste of the Maine woods could experience them in luxury hotels like the Mount Kineo House on Moosehead Lake and the Poland Spring House near Portland. Later on, as less well-to-do visitors discovered Maine, rustic cabins, known as camps, became the rage—cozy retreats in the middle of the rough outdoors.

By the early 1900s Maine had become such a popular vacation spot that some people worried it would soon be spoiled. So working with

In the early 1900s, residents from cities such as Boston and New York, vacationed in Maine to escape the heat of the city.

government officials, conservationists started making some of its most scenic areas into public preserves. The first big piece of land to be protected was Mount Desert Island, the craggy headland that forms the backdrop for Bar Harbor. The island was named a national monument in 1916, and in 1919 it became a national park, with the name Lafayette National Park. In 1929 the park, enlarged to include the tip of the Schoodic Peninsula, was renamed Acadia National Park.

THE TWENTIETH CENTURY AND BEYOND

Maine suffered with the rest of the nation during the Great Depression of the 1930s, when the economy crashed, factories closed, and farm prices tumbled. But its natural attractions flourished under a government work program known as the Civilian Conservation Corps (CCC). The CCC hired more than 20,000 men and women to build trails, roads, bridges, and camping shelters, opening Maine's woods to hikers. In 1937 it was a CCC crew that built the final stretch of the Appalachian Trail, which runs through the White Mountains.

When the United States entered World War II, citizens of Maine went to work building warships for the U.S. military. Old shipbuilding towns like Kittery and Bath got a new lease on life, as citizens constructed submarines and iron-clad destroyers. Bath Iron Works grew from a midsize plant with a few hundred workers to an industrial giant employing 12,000. But the state's textile mills and leather industries that once produced clothing and shoes for the soldiers were beginning to move to the southern states where they could make bigger profits. During the 1950s the number of small farms was drastically decreasing

In 1937 the final stretch of the Appalachian Trail, which runs through the White Mountains, was built by several hundred CCC workers.

as large farming operations took their place. This was when Maine potatoes started being produced on an industrial scale and would soon become one of Maine's most successful agricultural crops.

It was also around midcentury that the state legislature created tax laws that encouraged new industries to come to the state, such as the budding electronics businesses. Outside Andover a satellite station was built and in 1962 was the first capable of receiving television signals from France. Improvements to roads increased accessibility for tourists of the natural beauty that Mainers had known all their lives. Tourists then could visit Maine's modernized ski lodges in the winter as well as enjoy the rocky summertime shores.

In the 1980s environmentalists pressed Maine's government to pay attention to crucial issues involving natural resources. For example, as paper mills expanded in the state, so too did the pollution from paper production. Maine's waterways were suffering from toxic runoff. Environmental groups went into action, forcing the government to pass new laws. The paper mills were then forced to create better systems for disposing their waste, and the state enjoyed cleaner rivers.

In the mid–1990s, concerned about funding future conservation programs, Maine set aside a portion of the money the state gathered from the state lottery. These particular lottery tickets went on sale in 1996 and since that time, nearly 11 million tickets have been sold, bringing in more than $13 million in grants to almost five hundred different outdoor projects. Some of the programs that have been funded through these sales include work on Maine's portion of the Appalachian Trail, projects to improve the habitat of Maine's inland fisheries, and land trusts that are set up to protect the state's natural landscape.

As the twenty-first century progressed, some parts of Maine, such as the Portland area in the south, enjoyed a boom in tourism. But the northern half of the state was not so lucky. In fact, people sometimes said there are two Maines. The one in the south was modernizing and prospering, while the land in the north, was undeveloped and the economy was poor.

One of the main concerns of the twenty-first century, many Mainers believe, is to make sure that the bounty of this beautiful state is shared by all the residents, those upcountry as well as those living along its southern boundaries.

Chapter Three
Together in Maine

A person who wanted to make a general statement about the people in Maine would probably speak about the values of hard work, thrift, and honesty that are more important to Down East folks. Mainers are also known for speaking their minds without wasting a lot of words. Between their broad New England accents and their conservative attitudes, longtime Mainers can sometimes seem a bit rough around the edges to people visiting the state for the first time. But after getting to know them better, most out-of-staters find that even the most cranky Mainers are also remarkably tolerant, fair-minded, and kind.

NATIVES AND FLATLANDERS

With its old New England heritage Maine is anything but cosmopolitan. More than 96 percent of the state's residents are white. That means that only 3.3 percent of the population is of other ethnicities, such as African American, Hispanic, Asian American, or American Indian.

Kayaking down the Kennebec River on a hot summer day is a favorite pastime among Mainers.

But even if Maine isn't as diverse as some other states, that doesn't mean Mainers are all alike. Ask a few residents about their neighbors, and you'll begin to grasp the differences—even between people who look and act pretty much the same.

To start with Mainers make a big distinction between year-round residents and summer people. For more than a hundred years people from farther south have been coming to Maine to spend the summers. Some families have been vacationing in the same spot for generations, often buying homes in Maine. Locals have gotten used to their summer neighbors, and relations between the two groups are generally polite and easygoing. Still, the two groups usually keep to their separate worlds. Their differences can be a source of amusement, too. Year-round Mainers like to poke gentle fun of the overindulged city folks, while for summer people, the locals with their colorful accents are part of the reason they find their summer stays in Maine so charming.

Even being born in Maine and living there year-round doesn't necessarily make you a native in the minds of some old-time Mainers. Many communities are populated by members of families who have lived side by side for hundreds of years. When a new family moves in, it may take a generation or two before the neighbors think of them as locals. Instead, they'll likely be considered flatlanders, or people from away. Philadelphia native Ann Wilson's family moved to rural Maine when she was three. "If you're a kid and you come from someplace else," remembered Wilson, "you either become an object of fascination or you get called quee-ah—which means weird."

A native Mainer takes pride in his shipbuilding sills.

THE BEAR AND THE SLICKER

Down East humor sometimes targets summer visitors—and sometimes plays on the blunders of Mainers themselves. Who has the last laugh in this traditional tale?

A city slicker was asked to go hunting with a group of Maine sportsmen. When the slicker said he couldn't bring himself to kill a harmless deer, they gave him a squirrel gun and told him to go off and find a bear. He struck off bravely into the woods, and before ten minutes were gone, he came upon what he was looking for. He dropped his gun and tore back to camp with the bear close on his heels. The slicker tripped on the cabin doorsill, and the bear tripped on him, rolling head over heels into the cabin. The slicker got up, dashed outside, slammed the door behind him, and then, peering in the window, he shouted, "There's your bear, fellows. You skin him out while I go back for more!"

ETHNIC MAINE

The oldest Maine families with European roots are of English, Scottish, and French heritage. These people came to the area when it was still a frontier, and many still make their living the way their ancestors did—fishing, lumbering, lobstering, or farming.

In the mid–nineteenth century many people came to the state from poverty-stricken Ireland and Quebec, Canada, to find work in its mills and factories. These newcomers were not accepted at first. As Catholics they were

ETHNIC MAINE

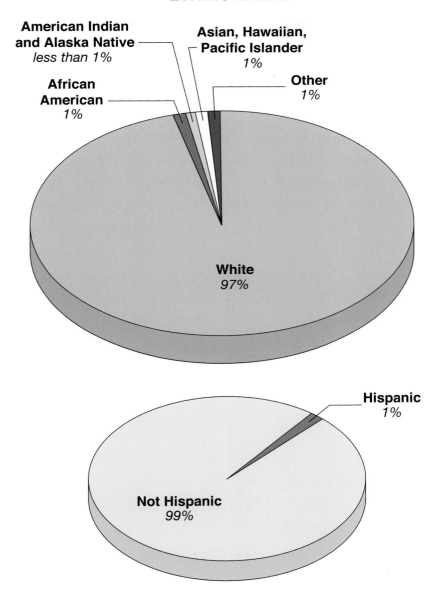

American Indian and Alaska Native *less than 1%*

Asian, Hawaiian, Pacific Islander 1%

Other *1%*

African American *1%*

White *97%*

Hispanic *1%*

Not Hispanic *99%*

Note: A person of Cuban, Mexican, Puerto Rican, South or Central American, or other Spanish culture or origin, regardless of race, is defined as Hispanic.

looked down on by the state's strong Protestant majority. In time, though, they became as much a part of Maine as the industries they supported.

Maine is also home to many Scandinavian Americans. Finns came to work in the granite and slate quarries along the coast in the nineteenth century. And in 1870, fifty-one Swedes helped set up a model farming community in Aroostook County. Their descendants still live in the town they founded, New Sweden, as well as in nearby Stockholm. Each June during New Sweden's Midsommar Festival, residents celebrate the longest day of the year the Swedish way, with colorful costumes, music, dancing, and a smorgasbord—a banquet featuring traditional Scandinavian foods.

Americans of French heritage make up Maine's largest non-British ethnic group, accounting for nearly one-fourth of the state's population.

UNE FÊTE ACADIENNE (CAJUN HOLIDAY)

Each year at the end of June the people of the Saint John River valley dance to the music of their French forebears during the most popular cultural celebration in Maine, Madawaska's Acadian Festival. While fiddlers play lively Franco-American tunes, visitors can sample local specialties like *ployes* (buckwheat cakes), *poutine* (french fries with cheese and gravy), and *fougère* (wild fiddlehead ferns). The *fête* (festival) is also a reunion of sorts, since Madawaska honors a local family each year and invites long-lost relatives to return to their roots for a few days of Acadian-style *joie de vivre* (enjoyment of life).

One of the many attractions at Maine's annual Swedish Colony Midsommar Festival is the New Sweden Little Folk Dancers, dancing around the raised maypole.

Although most French-speaking Mainers in mill towns like Lewiston and Biddeford trace their roots to Quebec, the oldest French communities go back to a different source. They were started by people from New Brunswick and Nova Scotia—colonies formed by France in the 1600s, when the land was still known as Acadia. Driven from their home by the British in 1755, many Acadians fled to the Saint John River valley, where they established farms on the meager soil. Acadian culture has survived in towns like Van Buren, Frenchville, Fort Kent, and Madawaska, where you can still hear French spoken in the streets.

AFRICAN AMERICANS IN MAINE

For all its variety Maine is still a predominantly "white" state, and that can make life a bit lonely for the African Americans who live there. African Americans make up only 0.8 percent of the population. Racial discrimination can be a problem, but many people of color say the worst issue they face is simple ignorance. Roy Partridge, an African-American Episcopal priest in Scarborough, lived in Maine for a couple of decades. "People will ask me almost once a month: 'Are you from Maine?'" says Partridge. "What you get to experience is people saying, 'You're the first person of color I've ever known.'"

Not many people are aware that African Americans have lived in Maine for more than three hundred years. The first blacks were brought to the state as slaves. Others came to Maine after fleeing slavery in the South. Many found jobs on farms, at the docks, and on the railroads. Others worked as lumberjacks or as domestic help in private homes. Gerald Talbot, former head of the Portland chapter of the National Association for the

UNDERGROUND RAILROAD IN MAINE

Not too many people associate Maine with the Underground Railroad, the network of safe houses where fugitive slaves, mostly from the South, could rest and hide. The Underground Railroad ran through such states as Pennsylvania, Ohio, and New York as well as Maine. There is a house in Gardiner, for instance, called the Brewer House. In the early 1830s Captain John Brewer and his wife offered shelter. The fugitive slaves often arrived by boat on the Kennebec River. After a few days of rest with the Brewers, the slaves would continue on their journey into Canada.

Another safe haven for slaves attempting to secure their freedom was in Blue Hill, near Penobscot Bay. The house, now called the Arcady Downeast Inn, was connected to a tunnel that led into the woods. The house also contains a so-called false room, which is concealed by a secret panel. The room was big enough to accommodate at least two people.

In Vassalboro a large home called the Farwell Mansion, owned by abolitionist Israel Weeks, was a part of the Underground Railroad. The house had a big cellar from which Weeks dug a tunnel 50 yards long, a distance sufficient to permit undetected exits through the backyard. There is also the Nason House in Augusta. Its owners used a bookcase to conceal a large room connected to a secret passage, through which fugitives could leave to begin the next leg of their journey.

Even though African Americans make up less than one percent of the state's population today, they have lived in Maine for more than three hundred years.

Advancement of Colored People (NAACP) and Maine's first African-American state legislator, can trace his family roots in Maine back five generations, to the mid–1700s. It was his story that inspired a documentary about black families in Maine called *Anchor of the Soul: The History of an African American Community in Portland, Maine*. One of the creators of this documentary, Shoshana Hoose, said she put up with a lot of teasing at first when she mentioned she was going to do a film about African Americans in Maine. Many people responded that in that case, the film would be very short. This turned out not to be true. Once Hoose started digging into the history of the black community, she found so much information that her documentary ended up being extended into three parts.

POPULATION DENSITY

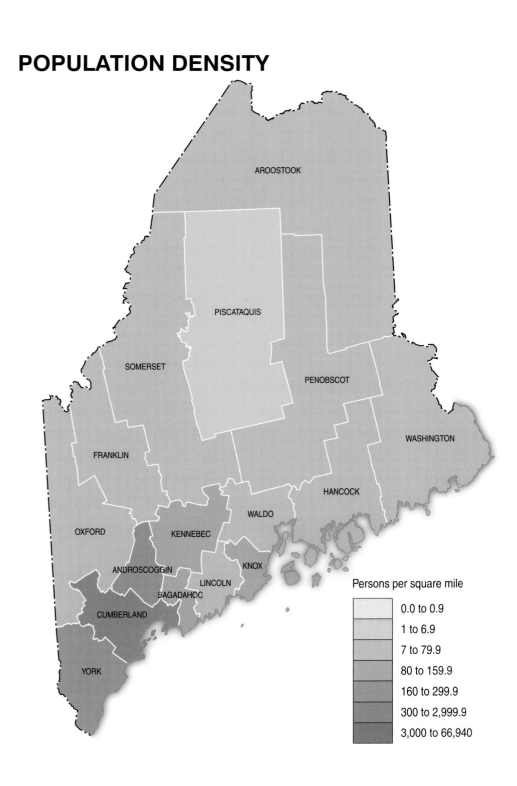

AROOSTOOK

PISCATAQUIS

SOMERSET

PENOBSCOT

FRANKLIN

WASHINGTON

OXFORD

KENNEBEC

WALDO

HANCOCK

ANDROSCOGGIN

KNOX

LINCOLN

SAGADAHOC

CUMBERLAND

YORK

Persons per square mile

0.0 to 0.9

1 to 6.9

7 to 79.9

80 to 159.9

160 to 299.9

300 to 2,999.9

3,000 to 66,940

AMERICAN INDIANS IN MAINE

Maine's American-Indian population has dwindled significantly over the centuries. In 2007 it was estimated to represent only 0.6 percent of the population. The remaining few can tell stories of their own hardships, including high rates of unemployment, alcoholism, and poverty. But these problems have eased since the Penobscot and the Passamaquoddy tribes went to court to demand payment for the 12.5 million acres they lost to Massachusetts in 1794. In a landmark decision in 1980 the tribes were awarded $81.5 million, the largest settlement of its kind in the United States. Since then conditions have improved on the tribes' reservations. There's also been a resurgence of interest in the cultures of tribal peoples. Older tribe members are helping children learn the Passamaquoddy language, for example. "We're working to keep our culture alive," said Joseph Nicholas. Each August the Passamaquoddy reservation at Pleasant Point, near Eastport, celebrates the tribe's heritage with Indian Days, a three-day festival featuring canoe races, crafts demonstrations, and traditional food and dance.

Today there are four Maine Indian tribes: the Maliseet, Micmac, Penobscot, and Passamaquoddy. Though native people live all over the state, much of the population lives in one of five recognized Indian reservations: the Indian Township, in Princeton; the Penobscot Reservation, in Old Town; Pleasant Point Passamaquoddy, in Perry; Aroostook Band of Micmac, on Presque Isle; and the Houlton Band of Maliseet, in Houlton.

A Micmac Indian farmer harvests blueberries, one of Maine's major crops.

HISPANIC AMERICANS IN MAINE

Hispanics make up the largest and fastest growing minority group, comprising a little more than one percent of Maine's population. Though Hispanic people live all around the state, the greatest percentage lives in Cumberland County on the southern coast. Besides the more permanent residents, there is also a large migrant Hispanic group, which has been estimated to be as large as 12,000 people, who come to the state to work each year. Many work in the fields, harvesting blueberries, apples, and other food crops. Others work in factories and processing plants.

BASKETS, FANCY AND STRONG

Most Maine American Indians live much as other Mainers do, and many of their grandparents' customs have been forgotten. But one Abenaki tradition is still alive and well—the ancient craft of basket making.

Centuries ago Maine's first residents learned to pound ash logs until the wood could be peeled off in flexible strips and woven together to make sturdy baskets. From the islands they gathered sweetgrass, a supple, fragrant plant that can be dried and twisted into delicate patterns for decoration. When city folk first began vacationing in Maine, Indian baskets became popular as knickknacks in summer homes. Penobscot and Passamaquoddy basket makers soon started shaping their wares to meet customers' needs, making all kinds of fancy items from pillboxes to picture frames. Larger undecorated baskets became the specialty of the Micmac and Maliseet, who sold them for use in fishing and potato harvesting.

Today a small community of Abenaki basket makers carries on the tradition, drawing on their own creativity as well as skills learned from older members of the tribe. Prized by collectors, their work commands a much higher price than the American Indians received at the end of the nineteenth century. But more important to most weavers is the chance to take part in a craft their families have passed down from generation to generation. As Passamaquoddy basket maker Sylvia Gabriel put it, "We all learned from one another."

Construction sites also often employ these migrant workers, most of whom come from Mexico. In the magazine called *Down East* Jeff Clark writes that even though some of these workers are in the state illegally, many of Maine's businesses would go broke without them.

Many Asian Americans in Maine are recent immigrants from such places as Vietnam and Cambodia. Although they make up almost as large a group as Hispanics, their population is growing less rapidly. Maine also has a small percentage of people from such African countries as Somalia, Ethiopia, and Sudan. Many of these most recent newcomers came to the United States to escape violent conflicts in their own countries and have been helped by a refugee resettlement program based in Portland. Before the 1970s Portlanders didn't have much contact with people from other parts of the world, so the growth of the city's international community has taken some adjustment on both sides.

At the same time a lot of Mainers appreciate the way immigration has changed the face of Portland. "I like standing on Congress Street and seeing all the different kinds of people walking by," said twenty-seven-year-old Sarah Bernhard. "People in African garb, Rastafarians, people speaking different languages. It's really great."

ISLAND LIFE

All over the Pine Tree State you'll find people who pride themselves on living in a remote, peaceful place far from the bothers of the city. But if you really want to know what solitude is all about, ask one of the estimated 4,700 people who live year-round on the state's offshore islands. Even the toughest Down Easters agree that island people are a breed apart—they

Some Mainers prefer to live on one of Maine's offshore islands.

pretty much have to be, considering the meager job prospects, severe winters, and physical isolation that the islands guarantee. The history of these island communities stretches back hundreds of years, but the decline in fishing and shipping has taken its toll on their populations in recent decades. Once there were three hundred Maine islands with full-time residents; now there are just fifteen.

The people who live on these last island outposts are known for their fierce independence. But they are also good at pulling together and helping each other get through the year. Some say that a strong feeling of community more than makes up for the loneliness of living offshore. New Jersey native Jackie Bell moved to Great Diamond Island in Casco Bay in 1993. She and her husband experienced the island's close-knit community during their very first week, when their electricity went out and five neighbors called to make sure they were okay. "We are deliriously happy here."

While a few island communities, like the one on Matinicus Island, still subsist by fishing and lobstering, most depend at least partly on business from summer residents. The population of Great Chebeague Island, for example, swells from 325 to about 2,000 in midsummer. The yearly influx not only brings jobs, it also makes things more lively for three months out of the year. "I love the winters here," said Alnah Robinson. "But come springtime, you're looking forward to seeing people again."

Chapter Four

Making Laws, Making a Living

A favorite Down East catchphrase says that Maine is "the way life should be." For summer visitors it's easy to agree. The state's fresh air, slow pace, and enchanting scenery can make it seem like a paradise to people who need to unwind from the stress of Boston or New York. But year-round Mainers do not always have the same ideas about what makes the state livable—or how to keep it that way. They have their own concerns, like improving education, creating job opportunities, and protecting the environment. Maine's government gives citizens a chance to decide what they want for their state and helps provide ways everyone can work together to make it happen.

INSIDE GOVERNMENT

Like the federal government, Maine's state government is divided into three branches: executive, legislative, and judicial.

The Maine State House in Augusta is a majestic structure built in the early 1800s using one of the state's plentiful resources, granite. It houses the senate and legislature.

AN EARLY POLITICAL FORCE—JAMES GILLESPIE BLAINE

James Gillespie Blaine was born in Pennsylvania, but he moved to Maine in 1854 as editor of the newspaper *Kennebec Journal* and later the *Portland Advertiser*. But his influence on the new state would take a different turn when five years later, Blaine became chairman of the state's Republican Party. It was his first step into politics, but he would retain party leadership for more than thirty years.

For the first twenty of those years Blaine held the chairman's post and was active in every election in the state in which Republican candidates ran. In addition, he served three terms in Maine's state congress, as a representative and later as the Speaker of the House. His name was well recognized as a driving force for the Republican Party. Though he was influential in giving his party a voice, his decades in Maine were just the beginning of a very long political career.

In 1863 Blaine was sent to Washington, D.C., after being elected as a U.S. representative. During his six terms he was once again honored with the post of Speaker of the House, this time on the federal level. He served in that position for the last six of his twelve years in Congress. At the end of his last term in the House of Representatives Blaine went home and rounded up enough votes to return to Washington as one of Maine's U.S. senators.

Blaine was known for his eloquence, which served him well during his years in Congress, especially through the conflicts of the Civil War and the Reconstruction Era that followed. In 1876 Blaine made an unsuccessful run for president as the Republican candidate. He lost because he was tarred by rumors of corruption that were never proven.

Executive

The executive branch carries out state laws. It is headed by the governor, who makes decisions with the help of a cabinet of experts on major public issues from education to the economy. Maine's governor is elected by the public every four years. The state's four other executive officers—secretary of state, attorney general, treasurer, and auditor—are elected by the legislature.

Legislative

The legislative branch makes laws and decides how the state should spend its money. Maine's legislature is made up of two houses: a senate with 35 members and a house of representatives with 151 members. Each member of the legislature is elected by the public for a two-year term.

The legislature's most important task is to create bills—proposals for new laws. After a bill has been approved in both the House and the Senate, it lands on the governor's desk. If the governor signs the bill, it becomes law. If the governor vetoes it, the bill dies, unless two-thirds of the members of both houses vote to override the veto.

Judicial

The judicial branch hears legal cases and interprets state law. Maine's judicial system has three levels. At the lowest level are thirteen district courts, where many types of minor criminal and civil cases are heard. At the second level is the sixteen-member Superior Court, where a justice and jury hear serious criminal cases and important civil cases. A person who is dissatisfied with a decision made by a lower court may appeal to the Superior Court to have the ruling reviewed. The Supreme Judicial Court is the highest level. It consists of a chief justice and six associate justices, whose main job is to hear cases appealed from lower courts. The governor appoints all judges on these courts to seven-year terms.

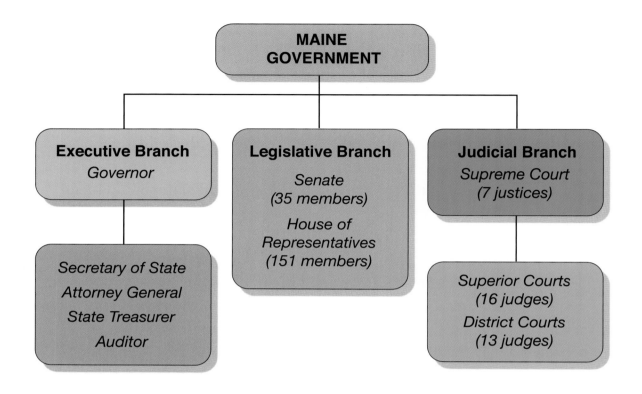

POLITICS IN ACTION

When it comes to politics, Mainers take pride in doing things their own way—even if it means bucking the nation's traditional two-party system. The Pine Tree State, for example, has a very active group of Independent voters in addition to the Democrats and Republicans. Independents often provide the swing vote that decides whether the Democratic or Republican candidate wins. But Independent politicians can also run on their party's ticket and win, as did James B. Longley, in 1974, and Angus S. King, in 1994. Both men were elected governor.

DEMOCRATS COME INTO POWER
IN MAINE POLITICS

The Republican Party had dominated politics in Maine for most of the previous one hundred years. That was until Edmund Muskie (below) appeared on the scene. The people of Maine elected him governor in 1954. It was through Muskie that the Democrats turned Maine into a true two-party state. Four years later Muskie was sent to Washington as a Maine senator. Like Blaine before him, Muskie took to national politics and brought attention to the state when he ran as Hubert Humphrey's vice-presidential candidate. Again like his predecessor Blaine, in 1979 Muskie was appointed secretary of state under Democratic president Jimmy Carter.

George J. Mitchell, another Democrat from Maine, ran for governor in 1974 but lost. Three years later he was appointed U.S. attorney for Maine. Then in 1979 he served as a federal district court judge. When Muskie retired from his U.S. Senate seat in 1980, Mitchell was appointed as his replacement. Two years later Mitchell won his own election and remained in Congress until 1995. That is when the Republicans won again, sending Olympia J. Snowe to the Senate. In 1997 Susan M. Collins, also a Republican, won the second Senate seat for Maine. Also in 2008 Mainers followed suit along with the other New England states and voted for Democratic presidential candidate Barack Obama. This was the fifth time in a row that Mainers voted for a Democratic president.

One Maine politician—a Democrat, in this case—made his greatest contribution after retiring from politics. After a distinguished career in the U.S. Senate, Waterville native George J. Mitchell was chosen to help find a solution to the long-running conflict between Protestant and Catholic factions in Northern Ireland. With his help, in 1998 the two sides signed a groundbreaking agreement that has since brought peace to this battle-weary land. A decade later Mitchell was appointed to the position of Special Envoy to the Middle East by President Barack Obama.

On April 10, 1998, British prime minister Tony Blair (right), U.S. state senator George J. Mitchell (center), and Irish prime minister Bertie Ahern (left) signed a historic agreement for peace in Northern Ireland, ending a thirty-year conflict.

MAINE BY COUNTY

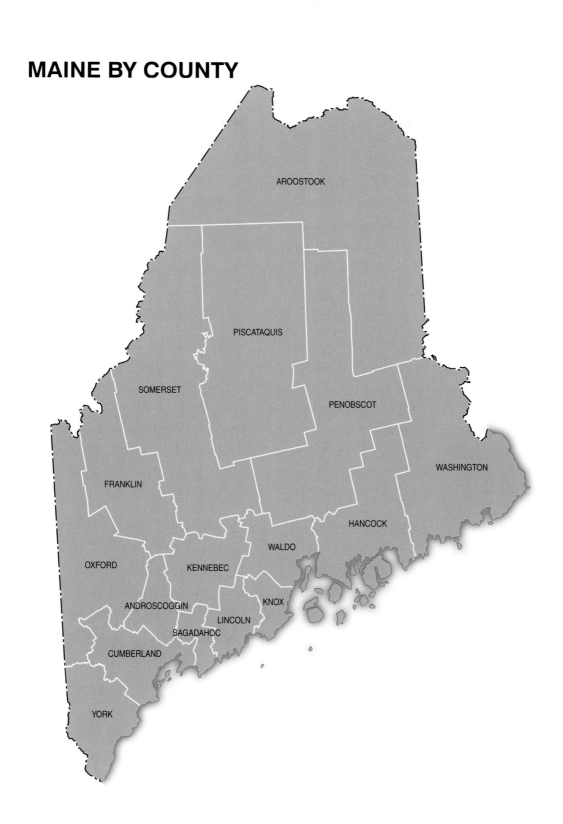

FINDING A BALANCE

A question dividing the state today is the same one that has challenged it for decades: How can Maine's natural resources be used in a way that brings the most benefit to everyone? Striking the right balance between providing jobs and preserving resources is not easy. The problem often pits environmentalists against people working in traditional industries like fishing and logging—and the debates can get pretty heated.

In the mid–1990s, for example, environmental groups raised a storm of controversy by circulating a petition for a statewide ban on clear-cutting, which is the removal of an entire standing crop of trees. More than 55,000 citizens signed it—enough to get the proposal on the ballot. "This really is a last-ditch effort to put brakes on the destruction of the north woods," said Jonathan Carter, a leading activist behind the measure.

But most people in the lumber and wood products industries were against the ban, predicting that business would suffer and thousands of workers would lose their jobs. Calling the proposal a "gun to the head of the Maine economy," Governor Angus King got together with industry leaders and tried to persuade Mainers to vote it down.

At the polls a majority of Mainers voted against the clear-cutting ban. They also rejected a compromise measure, which would have reduced clear-cutting without stopping it altogether. Today many people argue that clear-cutting is regulated enough already—around 5 to 10 percent of Maine's tree harvest is clear-cut these days. But that has not put an end to the controversy. In a state where thousands of people make a living from the woods—and where thousands more love to hike and camp—taking care of the forests is bound to remain a big public issue for years to come.

Harvesting Maine's lumber has left clean-cut holes in the state's forests.

Governor Angus King, before he left office in 2003, suggested that the state should buy laptop computers for every middle-school student in the state. This was a controversial topic, with even teachers questioning if this would benefit students. The plan went forward, and now more than 30,000 middle-school students and their teachers have laptops. The next step, according to a report in 2008, is to do the same for Maine's high schools.

Maine's government is helping to improve its schools by investing in up-to-date electronic equipment.

Through the Maine Writing Project, teachers who are considered technology-savvy train teachers on how to use the computers to increase their students' creativity, literacy, and technological skills. This, the Board of Education hopes, will especially help students in Maine's rural areas, such as those in the northern part of the state. Students are encouraged to create blogs and podcasts. They also learn how to do research online to help them develop stories. So far, teachers are reporting that their students' interest in writing has increased dramatically. Backing this up is a recent report from the University of Southern Maine, which confirmed that the program is succeeding. Another verification of the success of this program is the improvement of scores on the state's writing assessments.

By working together, Maine's people and the government representatives they have elected are creating a state that helps to preserve the environment, to strengthen the economy, and to ensure that every Mainer has the skills to persevere and thrive in the future.

Chapter Five
Maine's Economy

The Pine Tree State's economy surged in the 1980s as an increase in U.S. military spending boosted employment at two of Maine's biggest operations, the Bath and Kittery shipyards. But that boom was short-lived. In the early 1990s the U.S. government signed fewer shipbuilding contracts and closed Loring Air Force Base—northern Maine's largest employer. Stiff competition among world paper manufacturers made matters even worse. More than one hundred people lost their jobs when Kimberly-Clark in Winslow reduced production at its paper plant in 1996. The next year the plant closed down, laying off another 260 workers. "There's an old proverb," said Bruce Marshall, who was let go after working for the company for twenty-eight years. "Anything man has made never lasts. And it's true. Cars don't last. Buildings don't last. Jobs don't last. But how many times do we have to change our lifestyle to stay in the state of Maine . . . to survive?"

But things did get even worse. At the end of 2008 the nation was in the throes of an economic crisis, and Maine, like the rest of the country, found itself in a recession. More companies were laying off

The fishing industry remains a key source of income for Maine's economy. These fishermen look over their sea urchin catch.

employees, people were losing their homes, and the federal government was struggling to find a way to save U.S. banks from collapsing.

Maine's unemployment rate in mid–2009 was about 8 percent of the workforce (over 40,000 people). In the north the unemployment rate was around 4.8 percent, whereas in the south it was around 4.1 percent. The national rate was 8.1 percent. With over 10 million Americans officially out of work across the states, it was the highest unemployment rate in over five years. In 2009 neither economists in Maine nor those studying national trends predicted positive changes in the near future.

MAINE WORKFORCE

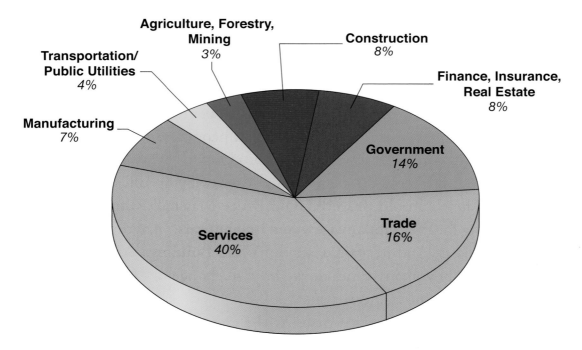

Agriculture, Forestry, Mining 3%

Construction 8%

Transportation/ Public Utilities 4%

Finance, Insurance, Real Estate 8%

Manufacturing 7%

Government 14%

Services 40%

Trade 16%

MAINE'S WATERS HELP TO KEEP THE ECONOMY ALIVE

Two historic Maine industries, fishing and lobstering, continued to support many of Maine's coastal towns through the years. By 2008, however, fewer people made a living from the sea than in the recent past. The populations of cod, flounder, haddock, and other fish typically found along the New England coast had sunk so low that strict limits were placed on the amounts fishing boats could bring in. Maine's Atlantic cod catch, for example, dropped 50 percent between 1985 and 1998. To help get the numbers back up again, in 1999 the New England Fishery Management Council slashed the daily cod allowance off the Gulf of Maine from 400 pounds to 200 pounds—putting a big dent in the coastal economy. By 2008 the cod population did not seem to be coming back in encouraging numbers, and scientists predicted that it was too late to restore the cod population to its former size.

Though many have made lobstering a way of life in Maine, biologists warn that lobster populations are in decline.

Biologists have also been warning lobstermen for years that their livelihood might disappear. But in 2007 Maine lobster traps took in more than 63 million pounds of lobster, though this was almost 12 million pounds less than the year before.

When many people think of Maine, it is often lobsters that come to mind. Lobsters were also on the mind of Senator Olympia Snowe when she made an appeal to the national legislature. In November 2008 Senator Snowe asked Congress to come to the aid of Maine's lobster business. Though lobsters were maintaining a healthy population size, Snowe pointed out some of the difficulties the industry was facing in the general economic downturn. "Maine's lobster industry is a fundamental part of the state's economy as well as its coastal culture and unique identity," said the senator. With the cost of fuel and bait rising at the same time that the price of lobsters was falling, making a living from catching and selling lobsters was becoming almost impossible.

ANOTHER OLD INDUSTRY IN MAINE—PAPER

The paper industry, an important ingredient in Maine's economy as well as one of the oldest, was also feeling its share of challenges in 2008. The industry has a long history in the state. Mainers have been making paper pulp since 1868. By 1880 Maine was proud to claim the largest paper mill in the world, the S. D. Warren Company in Westbrook. By 1890 there were twenty-five pulp mills in Maine, which produced 182 tons of pulp each day. Five years later Maine's capacity increased to 1,036 tons per day. Some of the biggest mills at this time were located in Gardiner, Mechanic Falls, Poland, Canton, Waterville, Norway, South Paris, and Brunswick.

The paper industry rapidly expanded as more mills were built, notably in Millinocket and Rumford, and faster production equipment was installed. But the competition was also growing, especially from mills located in Canada. The competition proved too stiff for some of Maine's

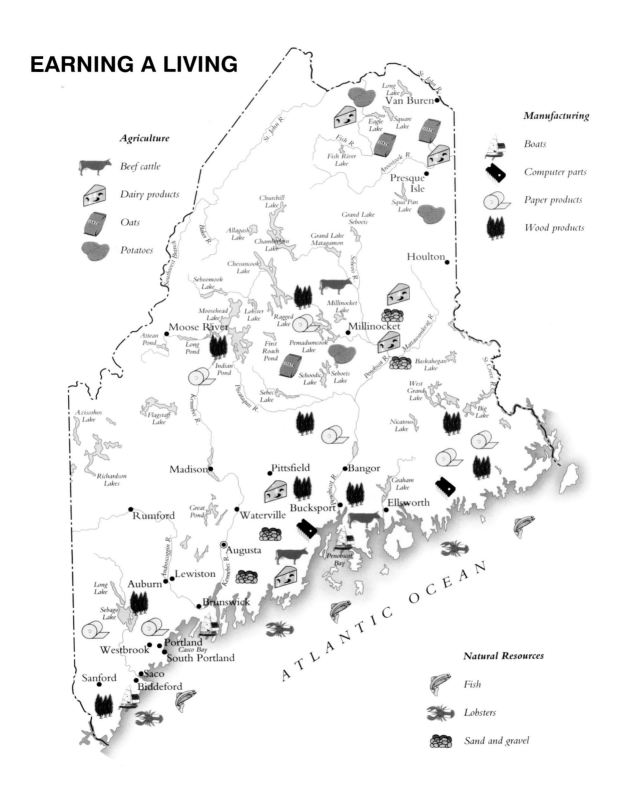

EARNING A LIVING

Agriculture

🐄 Beef cattle

🧀 Dairy products

OATS Oats

🥔 Potatoes

Manufacturing

Boats

Computer parts

Paper products

Wood products

Natural Resources

🐟 Fish

🦞 Lobsters

Sand and gravel

Van Buren
Long Lake
St. John R.
Eagle Lake
Square Lake
Fish R.
Fish River Lake
Aroostook R.
Presque Isle
Squa Pan Lake
Houlton
St. John R.
Churchill Lake
Allagash Lake
Chamberlain Lake
Grand Lake Seboeis
Grand Lake Matagamon
Seboeis R.
Chesuncook Lake
Seboomook Lake
Baker R.
Southwest Branch
Moosehead Lake
Lobster Lake
Ragged Lake
Millinocket Lake
Millinocket
Mattawamkeag R.
Baskahegan Lake
St. Croix R.
Attean Pond
Moose River
Long Pond
Indian Pond
First Roach Pond
Pemadumcook Lake
Schoodic Lake
Seboeis Lake
Penobscot R.
West Grand Lake
Big Lake
Aziscohos Lake
Flagstaff Lake
Kennebec R.
Piscataquis R.
Sebec Lake
Nicatous Lake
Graham Lake
Richardson Lakes
Madison
Great Pond
Pittsfield
Bangor
Rumford
Androscoggin R.
Waterville
Bucksport
Ellsworth
Augusta
Penobscot Bay
Kennebec R.
Lewiston
Long Lake
Auburn
Sebago Lake
Brunswick
ATLANTIC OCEAN
Westbrook
Portland
Casco Bay
South Portland
Sanford
Saco
Biddeford

Paper mills feed the economy, but also pollute the state's water and air.

paper companies, and they were forced to close. Other companies hung on and improved to the point that by 1930, Maine proudly claimed to be the second leading paper-producing state, behind New York. Thirty years later Maine would claim the top spot—the leading papermaking state in the nation. However, by the 1980s, Washington State knocked Maine back down to the second position.

During the 1990s competition from international companies in Europe, Latin America, and Asia increased. The newer mills produced paper faster and their products cost less money, forcing the price of paper down. To compete, Maine's paper mills had to both lay off workers and invest in better equipment. Many of the older paper mills had no choice but to completely close down.

Despite these challenges the industry remains competitive and represents the state's largest manufacturing sector. Though the industry is surviving, there are still many other challenges to overcome. One challenge comes from environmentalists, who are pressuring the companies to use the state's forests in a way that promotes sustainable growth, protects the natural habitats of wildlife, and guards the environment. The other challenge comes from what has been called the graying of the workforce. The average age of workers in the paper industry is fifty-four. And while many of these people will be retiring in the next decade, employers are having trouble attracting younger workers to the industry. Bill Cohen, spokesman for Verso Paper, which has mills in Bucksport and Jay, said that one of the reasons it is so difficult to get new recruits is "the perception that it is a dying industry." This perception, in turn, stems from the observation that the number of plants continues to decline, and paper companies continue to lay off workers.

TOURISM MAY CONTINUE TO GROW

Though Maine's economy was once highly dependent on manufacturing, in the past decades it has been moving toward the service industries, such as tourism. The Maine Department of Labor calls tourism Maine's primary industry. Coastal towns provide food, lodging, and transportation to summer vacationers, and western mountain towns host winter skiers and snowmobilers. Tourism can mean big money. In 2007 the industry

Thunder Hole, a tourist attraction in Acadia National Park, is a great place to experience the thunder of the sea against the rocky shores of Maine.

brought in more than $10 billion in sales of goods and services and provided about 140,000 jobs, whose workers earned $3 billion.

However, even the tourism industry has felt the effects of the 2008 recession. First, in the summer of 2008 gasoline prices skyrocketed, making it very expensive for people to drive to the state. Flying in also became more expensive as airlines passed on higher fuel costs to customers. But it wasn't just the economy that reduced the tourist population. A very cool summer, possibly due to global climate change, kept tourists away from the water. The mountains were even colder than usual. Economists, though, were predicting that Maine's tourism industry might escape many effects of the recession. Since Maine's neighbors include the big cities of New England, many who live there who are tightening their belts might find a drive to Maine (as long as the gasoline prices stay low) the most economical vacation they can get.

MAINE FARMING IS STILL ALIVE

Although Maine is not often thought of as an agricultural state, farmers there raise a lot of food. According to the Maine Department of Agriculture, the state farmers are stewards of 1.25 million acres and contribute $1.2 billion a year to the state's economy. The major agricultural products are brown eggs and wild blueberries.

The other big products are potatoes and maple syrup. Maine is ranked eighth in the country in the production of potatoes and second of maple syrup. Most of the maple syrup comes from Somerset County. Maine is also the second-largest producer of milk and livestock in New England. The majority of livestock is cattle, but farmers also raise sheep, goats, hogs, horses, and fowl. New animals have been added,

Maine ranks second in the country for the production of maple syrup.

though, and some are rather unusual for farms. These include state-licensed elk and deer herds, along with llama, alpaca, and emu—a large, ostrichlike bird.

NEW WAYS TO STIMULATE THE ECONOMY

As Mainers realize that the economic world is changing, they are looking for new industries to help create jobs. One of these new industries also suggests a way in which the state can wean itself from its dependency on oil. Specifically, many people in Maine are getting very serious about using wind power as an alternative source of energy.

According to the Maine Center for Economic Policy, the cost of electricity in New England has risen 55 percent since 1990. To offset this, some Mainers are looking to wind. One of those people is former governor Angus King, who has cofounded the company Independence Wind. Not only can wind power ease the cost of energy, both financially and environmentally, it can also create new jobs. Maine has the right geography to capture the wind, both on land and offshore. Some of the technology to do this has not yet been developed, but King believes things will fall into place in the not-too-distant future.

2007 GROSS STATE PRODUCT: $48 Million

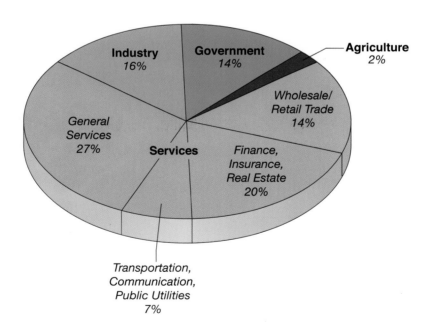

BLUEBERRY MUFFINS

Baked goods made from local blueberries are a popular treat in Maine, especially in the summertime. Have an adult help you make this recipe for a delicious Down East snack.

1 cup milk
1 egg
1/3 cup vegetable oil
2 cups all-purpose flour
2 teaspoons baking powder
1/2 cup sugar
1 cup blueberries (wild blueberries are the best!)

Preheat oven to 400 °F. Grease a twelve-cup muffin tin. Blend milk, egg, and oil in a large bowl. Add flour, baking powder, sugar, and blueberries and mix with just a few quick strokes. Don't overmix! That's the secret to great muffins.

Pour batter into muffin cups. Each cup should be about two-thirds full. Bake for twenty minutes, and serve fresh from the oven!

These days state leaders say attracting new businesses is the best way to keep the economy thriving, and that means Maine's economic makeup is destined to change. In some parts of the state you can see the shift taking place already. Telemarketing, Maine's fastest-growing industry, now employs many of the people who once worked in manufacturing. And Internet companies are starting up in the Portland area and along the coast.

One thing the state has going for it is a pleasant environment, which makes it appealing to companies as well as telecommuters—people who use the Internet to do business from home. Says one entrepreneur who recently moved from New York to Portland, "The fact is, this is a great place to live." There are a lot of people in Maine who would agree.

Chapter Six

Out and About in Maine

People who visit Maine in the summertime often end up going back year after year to the same spot, whether it's a lakeside camp or a fishing village on a quiet cove. But plenty of surprises await those who are willing to explore the state a bit more. An ideal place to start is in Maine's biggest city, Portland.

CITY BY THE SEA

Downtown Portland lies on a crooked peninsula jutting out into Casco Bay, an area the Abenaki called Machigonne, meaning "Great Neck." Portland's motto, *Resurgam*, is Latin for "I shall rise again." And indeed, the city has risen from near destruction several times. In 1690, during King Philip's War, French and Indian soldiers attacked the English settlement at Fort Loyal, beside Portland Harbor, and wiped out about forty families. The next onslaught came in 1775, when British warships leveled three-quarters of what was even then Maine's largest town.

The Burnt Island Lighthouse, just outside of Boothbay Harbor, is one of Maine's most popular tourist attractions.

After the American Revolution Portland sprang back to become stronger and more prosperous than ever before. It was during Fourth of July festivities in 1866 that the city met its third great disaster. While Portlanders reveled, a firecracker flew into a boatbuilder's yard and ignited a pile of wood shavings. Strong winds spread the blaze so quickly, it soon demolished most of central Portland. The red brick and granite buildings that make up the Old Port district now were built in the 1870s and 1880s, after the fire.

Today, Portland is a thriving city of nearly 63,000, combining a host of urban attractions with the easygoing atmosphere of a small town. Its historic downtown boasts dozens of great restaurants, shops, parks, and museums. From the cafes of the city's Old Port neighborhood you can stroll out to the end of a dock and watch ships and fishing boats navigate the waters of Casco Bay. For an even more spectacular view, you can board a ferry to one of the bay's lovely islands or take a sunset whale-watching cruise.

The state's oldest and most renowned art museum, the Portland Museum of Art, is just a few blocks away. Its State of Maine collection features paintings by Winslow Homer, Rockwell Kent, Maurice Prendergast, and Andrew Wyeth, all of whom created some of their best-known works while summering in Maine.

Portland's historic houses show how the wealthiest Mainers lived in days gone by. The Wadsworth-Longfellow House, built by the grandfather of Henry Wadsworth Longfellow in 1785, was the city's first brick house. A tour takes you through rooms furnished in the style of the early nineteenth century, when the poet was a young boy.

Portland Harbor, Maine's most traveled seaport, is a great place to take a sunset whale-watching cruise.

More lavish is the Victoria Mansion, also known as the Morse-Libby House, an 1850s summer residence displaying riches of stained glass, velvet, marble, and mahogany.

One thing people love about Portland is that even though it has the feel of a city, the country is always close by. Tucked amid the rolling hills of Cumberland County just to the north is a perfect example of old-fashioned farm life, the Sabbathday Lake Shaker Village in New Gloucester. The Shakers are members of a religious order formed in the 1700s. Sabbathday Lake, founded in 1783, is now the only active Shaker community in the world. Though they number fewer than ten, its members still honor the principles of simplicity, kindness, communal living, and equality that marked the Shakers' beginnings. A tour of Sabbathday Lake offers visitors a glimpse of life there in earlier times, when some of our most familiar household items, like the flat broom and the clothespin, were invented by Shaker craftsmen.

THE CAPITAL AND THE QUEEN CITY

Straddling the Kennebec River in the upland region is Maine's capital, Augusta. Government leaders meet under the copper dome of the Maine State House, whose original structure was built of local granite in 1832. Remodeled in the early twentieth century, it has some unusual features for a state capitol—including a stuffed moose and a bronze plaque left by Governor Percival P. Baxter in memory of Garry, his faithful red setter. Another Augusta landmark, Old Fort Western, was built in 1754 as part of the British expansion into the Kennebec Valley. A summer visit to the fort today may include demonstrations of frontier arts practiced at the fort during colonial times.

PLACES TO SEE

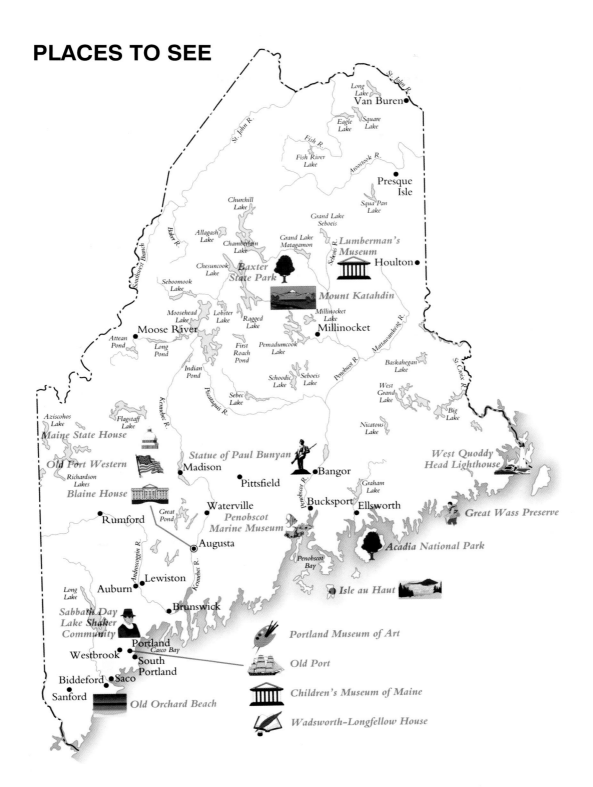

Van Buren

Long Lake
St. John R.
St. John R.
Eagle Lake
Square Lake
Fish R.
Fish River Lake
Aroostook R.

Presque Isle

Squa Pan Lake
Churchill Lake
Grand Lake Seboeis

Allagash Lake
Baker R.
Chamberlain Lake
Grand Lake Matagamon
Sebois R.

Lumberman's Museum
Houlton

Chesuncook Lake
Baxter State Park

Seboomook Lake
Mount Katahdin

Mattawamkeag R.

Southwest Branch
Moosehead Lake
Lobster Lake
Ragged Lake
Millinocket Lake
Millinocket

Moose River
Attean Pond
Long Pond
First Roach Pond
Pemadumcook Lake
Penobscot R.
Baskahegan Lake
St. Croix R.

Indian Pond
Schoodic Lake
Seboeis Lake
West Grand Lake
Big Lake

Piscataquis R.
Sebec Lake

Aziscohos Lake
Flagstaff Lake
Kennebec R.
Nicatous Lake

Maine State House
Statue of Paul Bunyan
West Quoddy Head Lighthouse

Old Fort Western
Madison
Pittsfield
Bangor
Graham Lake

Richardson Lakes
Blaine House
Waterville
Buckport
Ellsworth
Great Wass Preserve

Rumford
Great Pond
Penobscot Marine Museum
Acadia National Park

Androscoggin R.
Augusta
Penobscot Bay

Lewiston
Kennebec R.
Isle au Haut

Long Lake
Auburn
Brunswick

Sabbath Day Lake Shaker Community

Portland
Casco Bay
Portland Museum of Art

Westbrook
South Portland
Old Port

Biddeford
Saco
Children's Museum of Maine

Sanford
Old Orchard Beach
Wadsworth-Longfellow House

Not far from the center of downtown Bangor stands a thirty-one-foot statue of the legendary giant lumberjack Paul Bunyan. It was lumber, after all, that earned Bangor the nickname Queen City in the nineteenth century, and locals claim the world's biggest logger was a real-live Mainer, born in Bangor on February 13, 1834. Elegant mansions built by lumber barons still grace the town's streets. One of the finest, protected by a wrought-iron gate bedecked with bats and cobwebs, belongs to best-selling horror novelist Stephen King.

A trip to Bangor, Maine, would not be complete without driving by the elegant mansion of the famous horror writer Stephen King.

DOWN EAST

A stunning section of the Maine coast can be found just south of Bangor on the Blue Hill Peninsula, overlooking Penobscot Bay. For a taste of old-fashioned island life, take the mail boat from the old granite-quarrying town of Stonington to scenic Isle au Haut. Half of this island belongs to Acadia National Park; the rest is shared by locals and summer residents. On the park side, hiking trails will take you through the woods and along the shore, from one beautiful cove to another. Sit on a rock overlooking the ocean, listen to the waves, and watch the lobster buoys bob in the glittering water.

The main part of Acadia lies farther northeast, on Mount Desert Island. Covering more than 40,000 acres of woods, lakes, campgrounds, hiking trails, and rocky summits with dizzying views, this rugged playground attracts tourists all summer long. A great way to avoid big crowds is to walk or bike the carriage roads—a network of winding gravel paths that crisscross the park's eastern side. Some paths lead to the top of Cadillac Mountain. Others take hikers up more secluded peaks, like Beech Mountain, or toward dramatic sights, like Somes Sound, a narrow cleft that nearly cuts the island in two.

On the northeast side of Mount Desert lies the old resort town of Bar Harbor. Before the Civil War this was a sleepy fishing village called Eden. These days it's a mass of restaurants and motels. Most of the extravagant cottages that adorned Bar Harbor at the turn of the century were destroyed by a devastating fire in 1947. But here and there you can still see traces of the estates where wealthy families like the Du Ponts and the Vanderbilts entertained.

At the top of Cadillac Mountain, a hiker takes in the view.

Few tourists travel beyond Acadia to Washington County, Maine's loneliest stretch of shore. This unspoiled landscape of blueberry barrens, seaside villages, and rocky coastline spreads north and east to Cobscook Bay and the Canadian border. Near the sardine-fishing town of Lubec, red-and-white-striped West Quoddy Head Lighthouse stands guard over the easternmost spot in the United States, an eighty-foot-high cliff perfect for spotting whales. A bit further north, waters from the Saint Croix River wrestle with the area's drastic tides to create the whirlpool called the Old Sow, which is sometimes visible from the ferry between Eastport and Deer Island, New Brunswick.

The West Quoddy Head Lighthouse in Lubec is one of many along Maine's rocky shoreline.

A COUNTRY FAIR

One of the state's oldest agricultural fairs takes place each Labor Day weekend in the town of Blue Hill. It's a place where farm kids show off their best sheep, goats, cattle, and fowl, and oxen compete in load-pulling contests. With harness racing, a midway, a pig scramble, and a wild blueberry pie-eating contest, the Blue Hill Fair sticks to down-home fun. It's one Maine tradition that's changed very little over the years. In 1938 *New Yorker* writer E. B. White bought a farmhouse on Allen Cove, near Blue Hill. He quickly took to country life, and livestock shows at the Blue Hill Fair helped inspire his classic children's novel *Charlotte's Web*.

THE COUNTY

Aroostook County, the largest in the state, takes its name from a Maliseet word meaning "shining river." Mainers often just call Aroostook the County. Entering its wide-open spaces from the northeast coast means passing through the land where 90 percent of Maine's potatoes are grown. At Fort Fairfield's Potato Blossom Festival, held each July, locals celebrate the crop with a parade, mashed-potato wrestling, and a public potato supper, all surrounded by a sea of white, pink, and lavender blooms.

TEN LARGEST CITIES

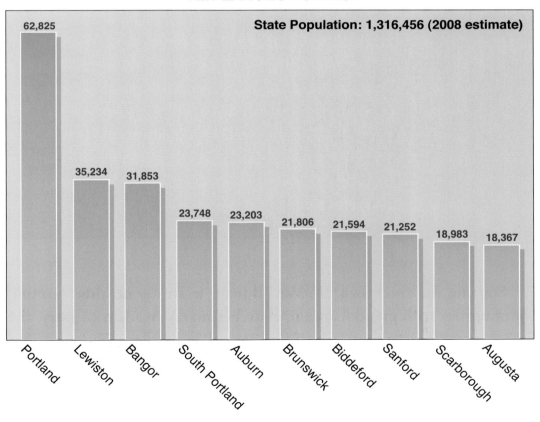

State Population: 1,316,456 (2008 estimate)

City	Population
Portland	62,825
Lewiston	35,234
Bangor	31,853
South Portland	23,748
Auburn	23,203
Brunswick	21,806
Biddeford	21,594
Sanford	21,252
Scarborough	18,983
Augusta	18,367

BEAN-HOLE BEANS

Tourists may rave about lobster and blueberry pie, but to Mainers, nothing says summer more than a Saturday-night supper of bean-hole beans. The cooking method for this delicious dish goes back to the Penobscot Indians, who prepared their food this way in colonial times.

On Friday afternoon the cook digs a hole in the ground a couple of feet deep, lights a wood fire in the bottom, and gives the beans a quick boil in an iron pot while the blaze dies down to glowing embers. After the beans have been flavored with salt pork, mustard, and molasses, the pot goes into the hole with a lid on top, gets covered with dirt, and sits overnight and all the next day. At about 5 p.m. on Saturday, the beans, baked to perfection, are carefully dug up and served.

Most small towns in Maine host public suppers featuring beans cooked in a hole in the ground. For a few dollars you can try them yourself and see if you agree that nothing compares to the taste of bean-hole beans.

Starting in the town of Van Buren, a string of tidy farming communities with grand Catholic churches marks Acadian country, the French-speaking region of the Saint John River valley. With its signs written in both French and English and French customs observed locally, this part of the state has a different flavor from any other—residents call it *chez nous* (our place). On the bank of the Saint John River near Madawaska, a 14-foot marble cross marks the spot where the Acadian founders first landed after their journey from Nova Scotia.

FORESTS, LAKES, AND STREAMS

It can take quite a while to get from the top of the state to Baxter State Park, in the center—miles and miles of forest cover the land in between. A good stopping place, the Lumbermen's Museum in Patten, shows what life used to be like for the men who harvested this vast timberland. The museum's nine buildings contain everything from life-size logging camps to giant saws to sleds for dragging logs through deep winter snows. Photographs of grizzled lumbering crews tell of the high risk and hard labor behind the boom years of the nineteenth century, when Bangor sent more than 8 billion board feet of timber around the world.

Life can still be pretty rugged to the west of here, in the untamed wilderness of Baxter State Park. A narrow dirt road takes you from one end of the park to the other. No pets, radios, or cell phones are allowed, and visitors have to bring in their own drinking water. The rules are strict, but because they are, there's no better place to experience the Maine woods. If you make arrangements ahead of time with a park ranger, you can hike up to a lake where you can rent a canoe, paddle across, and then hike on to a waterfall before hiking and canoeing back again. Stay quiet, and you might meet a moose along the way.

It takes a full day to hike Mount Katahdin, but those who do it are rewarded with unbelievable views. Writer Henry David Thoreau

Katahdin Stream Falls in Baxter State Park is one of Maine's many scenic landscapes.

never made it to the top, but from above the treeline, he marveled at the scene below: "I could see the country eastward, boundless forests, and lakes, and streams, gleaming in the sun. . . . Now and then some small bird of the sparrow family would flit away before me, unable to command its course, like a fragment of the gray rock blown off by the wind."

With forty-six mountain peaks and 175 miles of hiking trails, you could spend a whole lifetime exploring Baxter. But our tour ends here, at the Mountain of the People of Maine.

THE FLAG: *The state flag depicts the state seal against a blue background. The flag was adopted in 1909.*

THE SEAL: *The state seal shows a farmer and a seaman, who represent agriculture, fishing, and shipping, three important industries in Maine. Between them is a shield depicting a pine tree and a moose, which symbolize the state's forests and wildlife. The state seal was adopted in 1820.*

State Survey

Statehood: March 15, 1820

Origin of Name: Perhaps from the term *mainland*. Early explorers called the mainland the Main to distinguish it from offshore islands.

Nickname: Pine Tree State

Capital: Augusta

Motto: *Dirigo* (I lead)

Bird: Chickadee

Flower: White pine cone and tassel

Tree: White pine

Fish: Landlocked salmon

Insect: Honeybee

Gemstone: Tourmaline

Animal: Moose

Chickadee

White pine cone and tassel

STATE SONG

This rousing march was adopted as the official state song in 1937.

Words and Music by Roger Vinton Snow

GEOGRAPHY

Highest Point: 5,268 feet above sea level, at Mount Katahdin

Lowest Point: sea level along the coast

Area: 33,128 square miles

Greatest Distance North to South: 311 miles

Greatest Distance East to West: 202 miles

Bordering States: New Hampshire to the southwest

Hottest Recorded Temperature: 105 °F at North Bridgton on July 10, 1911

Coldest Recorded Temperature: −48 °F in Van Buren on January 19, 1925

Average Annual Precipitation: 41 inches

Major Rivers: Allagash, Androscoggin, Kennebec, Machias, Penobscot, Saco, Saint Croix, Saint John

Major Lakes: Chesuncook, Flagstaff, Millinocket, Moosehead, Pemadumcook, Rangeley, Sebago

Trees: balsam fir, basswood, beech, black ash cedar, hemlock, maple, oak, pine, spruce, white birch, yellow birch

Wild Plants: anemone, aster, bittersweet, black-eyed Susan, buttercup, goldenrod, harebell, hepatica, jack-in-the-pulpit, lady's slipper, lavender, mayflower, wild lily

Animals: beaver, black bear, bobcat, harbor seal, lynx, marten, mink, moose, porcupine, raccoon, red fox, white-tailed deer

Birds: bunting, duck, grackle, loon, osprey, owl, sparrow, spruce grouse, swallow, thrush, wren

Fish: alewife, bass, brook trout, cod, flounder, hake, mackerel, perch, pickerel, pollock, landlocked salmon, tuna

Endangered Animals: Atlantic salmon, eastern cougar, finback whale, humpback whale, leatherback sea turtle, right whale, roseate tern, shortnose sturgeon

Endangered Plants: Furbish's lousewort

Leatherback sea turtle

TIMELINE

c. 2500 BCE Paleo-Indians live in what is now Maine.

c. 1000 CE Vikings from Norway visit Maine.

1400s Abenaki, Passamaquoddy, Penobscot, Maliseet, and Micmac Indians live in what will become Maine.

1498 Explorer John Cabot reaches the Maine coast.

1604 Frenchman Samuel de Champlain explores and names Mount Desert Island.

1607 English colonists establish a settlement in Maine at the mouth of the Kennebec River; it is abandoned the following year.

1620s The English begin settling in Maine.

1631 Maine's first sawmill is constructed.

1677 Massachusetts gains control of Maine.

1775 The American Revolution begins; the first naval battle of the war takes place off Machias on the Maine coast.

1785 Maine's first newspaper, the *Falmouth Gazette*, begins publication.

1794 Bowdoin College, the first college in Maine, is established in Brunswick.

1819 Mainers vote to separate from Massachusetts.

1820 Maine becomes the twenty-third state.

1832 The state capital is moved from Portland to Augusta.

1833 Bath Iron Works opens.

1836 Maine's first railroad is built.

1842 The Webster-Ashburton Treaty ends a dispute over the border between Canada and Maine.

1851 Maine outlaws the manufacture and sale of alcohol, the only state to do so until 1934.

1861–1865 About 70,000 Mainers serve in the Union army during the Civil War.

1866 A fire destroys much of Portland.

1919 Acadia National Park is established and is called Lafayette National Park until 1929.

1923 Mainer Edna St. Vincent Millay wins the Pulitzer Prize for Poetry.

1927 Maine elects its first women to the state senate, Dora Pinkham and Katherine C. Allen.

1931 Baxter State Park is established.

1941 The United States enters World War II.

1948 Mainer Margaret Chase Smith becomes the first woman elected to the U.S. Senate.

1969 Maine enacts a state income tax.

1972 Gerald Talbot becomes the first African American elected to the state legislature.

1980 The Passamaquoddy and Penobscot Indians receive more than $80 million for land seized illegally in the eighteenth and nineteenth centuries.

1984 Joan Benoit Samuelson, born in Cape Elizabeth, becomes the first gold medal winner in the first women's Olympic marathon event at the Summer Olympics.

1999 Edwards Dam is removed in an effort to restore fish populations in the Kennebec River.

2000 Maine legislators pass a bill to lower all prescription drug prices, the first state to do so.

2003 The U.S. Supreme Court rules against pharmaceutical companies and upholds Maine's right to lower prices on prescription drugs.

2006 John Baldacci is elected to a second term as governor of Maine.

2008 Bangor is named eighth-safest city in the United States by a Washington, D.C., study.

ECONOMY

Agricultural Products: apples, beef cattle, blueberries, chickens, eggs, hay, milk, oats, potatoes

Manufactured Products: boats, electrical components, food products, leather products, lumber, paper products

Natural Resources: clams, fish, forests, granite, limestone, lobsters, sand and gravel

Blueberries

Business and Trade: banking, insurance, real estate, telemarketing, tourism, wholesale and retail trade

CALENDAR OF CELEBRATIONS

New Year's Portland Thousands of Portlanders bundle up warmly and head out on New Year's Eve to enjoy music, dance, and comedy performances and a big fireworks display at midnight.

U.S. National Toboggan Championships Hundreds of teams from around the country race down a 400-foot chute at the toboggan championships in Camden each February.

Maine Maple Sunday All across the state on the fourth Sunday in March, sugarhouses making maple syrup invite visitors in to enjoy the tasty treat.

U.S. National Toboggan Championships

Old Port Festival Portland is filled with music each June, when more than ten stages are set up, each for a different type of music. Festivalgoers can listen to smooth jazz for a while and then take in some foot-stomping country. Besides all the music, you might want to check out the parade, which has lots of musicians and puppets, and try your hand at some games.

Annual Windjammer Days You can get a feel for what Maine looked like in centuries gone by when tall ships sail into Boothbay Harbor each June. Besides watching the graceful old vessels, you can take in a concert, a dance, and fireworks, and maybe even tour a navy boat.

Annual Windjammer Days

La Kermesse Festival One of the nation's largest celebrations of Franco-American culture happens in Biddeford each June. A fireworks display starts off the event with a bang, and then there's a big parade. You might also want to try such traditional foods as crepes (thin pancakes), tourtière (pork pie), and boudin (blood sausage).

Great State of Maine Air Show
Each July 200,000 people show
up in Brunswick to watch some
of the nation's best stunt-flying
teams. The show also includes
displays of dozens of military
aircraft. You can even sit in the
cockpit of some of them.

Maine Lobster Festival Eat your
fill of Maine's favorite food each
August at what may be the world's
largest lobster feed in Rockland.
There's also a parade and a
rollicking clam-shucking contest
and race across lobster crates.

Great State of Maine Air Show

Maine Festival Musicians and dancers from around the nation and food
from around the world will vie for your attention at this four-day
August extravaganza in Brunswick.

Wild Blueberry Festival Mid-August is harvesttime for the wild
blueberries that grow near Machias. At this festival you'll end up with
a full stomach and blue lips.

Great Falls Balloon Festival Dozens of huge hot air balloons set sail
around Lewiston each August. If you want to get into the air yourself,
balloon and helicopter rides are available.

Harvestfest At this old-fashioned festival in York Village in October, you can enjoy an ox roast, hay rides, and lots of music.

Christmas Prelude Santa arrives in a lobster boat at this December event in Kennebunkport that kicks off the holiday season. Fairgoers can also eat their fill at a pancake breakfast, enjoy some caroling, and then tour the picturesque town.

STATE STARS

L. L. Bean (1872–1967), who founded one of the nation's leading outdoor gear retailers, was born in Greenwood. Early on, Bean became famous for the Bean boot, a shoe he devised with a rubber bottom and leather top, which is both lightweight and keeps your feet dry. Over the years so much of Bean's business came from catalog orders that his store eventually got its own zip code. Today, shoppers look to L. L. Bean for comfortable, casual clothing as well as outdoor gear.

William Cranch Bond (1789–1859) was an early leader in American astronomy. Bond began his career as a clockmaker, but an eclipse of the sun in 1806 captured his imagination. In 1839 he established the Harvard College Observatory in Massachusetts, which became a center of astronomical research during his many years as director there. Bond is credited with discovering the dark inner ring of the

William Cranch Bond

planet Saturn, as well as Hyperion, one of Saturn's moons. He also improved photography techniques for astronomy, taking the first photos of stars and better shots of the moon than ever before. Bond was born in Falmouth.

Robert Tristram Coffin (1892–1955), a poet from Brunswick, earned the 1936 Pulitzer Prize for Poetry for his book *Strange Holiness*. In his poetry he often described the sights, sounds, and people of the Maine seacoast. Coffin also wrote an autobiography, *Lost Paradise*, about his Maine boyhood.

William Cohen (1940–   ), a native of Bangor, served on the Bangor City Council before Mainers sent him to Congress in Washington, D.C., in 1973. When President Bill Clinton elected him for the job of secretary of defense, in 1997, Cohen, a strong supporter of the military, became the first Republican nominated to the position of secretary of defense by a Democrat.

William Cohen

Cyrus H. K. Curtis (1850–1933), a Portland native, founded the Curtis Publishing Company, which produced such magazines as the *Saturday Evening Post* and *Ladies' Home Journal*. Curtis started his publishing career at age fifteen, when he began putting out a four-page weekly called *Young America*. His first big success came in 1879, when he began publishing *Tribune and Farmer*. Four years later he started printing the paper's women's page separately as *Ladies' Home Journal*, a spinoff that became one of the nation's most popular magazines. Curtis later bought such newspapers as the *Philadelphia Public Ledger* and the *Philadelphia Inquirer*.

Dorothea Dix (1802–1887) was a social reformer who worked to improve the treatment of prisoners and the mentally ill. Dix became interested in these causes in 1841, when she began teaching Sunday school for women inmates at a prison and was horrified by the conditions there. She discovered that many of the prisoners were mentally ill and that they were often chained and beaten. Dix began campaigning for changes in the treatment of the mentally ill. Because of her efforts, institutions for the mentally ill were established in twenty states and Canada. Her work also resulted in major prison reforms in Europe. Dix was born in Hampden.

Dorothea Dix

Marsden Hartley (1877–1943) was an artist from Lewiston who often painted Maine landscapes. In 1912 Hartley went to Europe. Influenced by the artists there, he became one of the first Americans to make abstract paintings rather than works that show specific objects or scenes. By 1920 he was again painting pictures of Maine, but in a different way. In his later works the people and places were simplified, with strong outlines and bold colors. Among the most famous of these is his 1941 painting *Lobster Fishermen*.

Winslow Homer (1836–1910) was among the greatest nineteenth-century American painters. Born in Boston, Homer spent some of his childhood in Maine. Early in his career he often painted pleasant scenes of children and farm life. But he is most famous for the intense seascapes and fishermen he painted after moving to Prouts Neck on the Maine coast in 1883. These paintings often have dramatic contrast between dark and light and show people struggling against the power of nature.

Winslow Homer

Sarah Orne Jewett (1849–1909) wrote colorful but honest stories about rural Mainers. Jewett was born in South Berwick, the scene of many of her stories. Her books include *The Country of the Pointed Firs* and *Deephaven*.

Stephen King (1947–　), perhaps the world's most widely read horror novelist, is a brilliant storyteller who produces spellbinding novels year after year. King often writes about everyday situations that turn terrifying. In his first novel, *Carrie*, a high school girl uses her supernatural powers to get revenge on classmates. *Carrie*, *The Shining*, *Misery*, and many of King's other books have been turned into popular films. King was born in Portland.

Henry Wadsworth Longfellow (1807–1882) was one of the most popular poets of the nineteenth century. Using clear, simple language and musical rhythms, Longfellow wrote such classics as "Paul Revere's Ride" and *The Song of Hiawatha*. He was born in Portland and attended Bowdoin College.

Henry Wadsworth Longfellow

Hiram Maxim (1840–1916), an inventor from Sangerville, designed the first practical automatic machine gun, as well as an automatic sprinkler and an electric current generator. Some of Maxim's early inventions involved electric lights. After losing a lawsuit over a patent to Thomas Edison, the man credited with inventing the electric lightbulb, Maxim moved to England. Later in his career he experimented with building internal combustion engines for cars and planes.

Stephen King

Edna St. Vincent Millay
(1892–1950) won the
1923 Pulitzer Prize for
Poetry for *The Ballad of
the Harp Weaver*. Millay
was known for using
traditional poetic forms to
express strong emotions
about love and death. In
her later works Millay
showed more interest
in history. For instance,
the poems in her 1937
collection *Conversation at
Midnight* deal with events
that would lead to World
War II. Millay was born
in Rockland.

Edna St. Vincent Millay

George J. Mitchell (1933–   ) is a politician from Waterville. After
practicing law and sitting as a judge, Mitchell was elected to the
U.S. Senate in 1980. He retired in 1995 but did not stay out of the
public eye for long. Instead, he was tapped to chair peace talks in
Northern Ireland, where Protestant and Catholic factions had long
been in conflict. With his patience and willingness to listen, he became
trusted by all parties and was able to hammer out a treaty in 1998 that
brought the hope of peace to the war-torn region.

Edmund Muskie (1914–1996) was the first Democrat Mainer ever elected to the U.S. Senate. Muskie, a native of Rumford, served in the Maine House of Representatives and as the state's governor before being elected to the U.S. Senate in 1958. In 1968 Muskie was chosen as the Democratic vice-presidential candidate, but the Republicans won that year. Throughout his career Muskie was known for fighting pollution and promoting education.

Louise Nevelson

Louise Nevelson

(1899–1988) was an artist renowned for her abstract wooden sculptures. Nevelson worked in many styles and materials before making her most famous works in wood in the 1950s. She is best known for her so-called sculptural walls, boxes that were stacked and contained objects such as wheels and chair slats. Nevelson was born in Ukraine and moved with her family to Rockland in 1905.

Joan Benoit Samuelson (1957–   ), a native of Cape Elizabeth, won the first women's Olympic marathon at the 1984 games in Los Angeles. Benoit's first major marathon victory came in 1979 when she captured the prestigious Boston Marathon. She triumphed again in Boston in 1983 in world-record time. The year after winning Olympic gold, Benoit earned the James E. Sullivan Memorial Award for the nation's outstanding amateur athlete.

Margaret Chase Smith (1897–1995) was the first woman to be elected to both the U.S. House and the U.S. Senate. Smith, a Republican born in Skowhegan, entered the House in 1940 and was elected to the Senate in 1948. She became highly respected for speaking out against anything she viewed as extremist. For example, she was one of the first senators to oppose Senator Joseph McCarthy, who was making unsupported claims against people he said were communists. In 1964 Smith made history again when she became the first woman to vie for a major party's presidential nomination.

Margaret Chase Smith

Joan Benoit Samuelson

Gerald Talbot (1931–   ) was born in Bangor and can trace his Maine ancestry back to the Revolutionary War. He graduated from Bangor High School, joined the army, and worked for most of his life in the publishing industry. But he is best known for his work as an activist in the civil rights movement. In 1972 Talbot became the first African American elected to the Maine State Legislature. He went on to become a leading researcher of African-American and civil rights history in the state. In 1995 he donated his collection of papers and artifacts, called the African-American Collection of Maine, to the University of Southern Maine.

E. B. White (1899–1985) wrote the classic children's books *Charlotte's Web*, *Stuart Little*, and *The Trumpet of the Swan*. He was also one of America's most influential essayists, writing simple, elegant, and amusing pieces for such prestigious magazines as *The New Yorker* and *Harper's*. White, who was born in New York, moved to Allen Cove in 1938.

Kate Douglas Wiggin (1856–1923) wrote *Rebecca of Sunnybrook Farm*, a classic novel about a spirited girl from a poor family. The novel is set in a village very similar to Hollis, Maine, the town where Wiggin grew up. Besides writing, Wiggin also worked to improve the education of America's children. In 1878 she established the first kindergarten on the West Coast, and two years later she founded the California Kindergarten Teacher Training School.

E. B. White

Andrew Wyeth (1917–2009) was an artist who often painted landscapes of Maine. Wyeth, the son of painter and illustrator N. C. Wyeth, was born in Pennsylvania but during his childhood spent his summers in Maine. As an adult he lived in Cushing. Wyeth's realistic paintings, which are often bathed in browns and grays, are immensely popular. In 1970 he became the first living artist to have an exhibition at the White House. One of his most famous works, *Her Room*, hangs in the Farnsworth Museum in Rockland, Maine.

Andrew Wyeth

TOUR THE STATE

Old Gaol Museum (York) You can visit the jail cells where some of Maine's earliest criminals were kept. Built in 1719, it is the oldest English public building in Maine.

Old Orchard Beach (Old Orchard Beach) After relaxing on the fabulous sandy beach, you might want to head up to the amusement park and pier for some rides and games.

Old Orchard Beach

Seashore Trolley Museum (Kennebunkport) Hop on a historic trolley for a 4-mile ride. Then take a look at some of the 250 other trolleys from around the world housed in this unusual museum.

Penobscot Marine Museum (Searsport) This fascinating museum includes several historic buildings, including a sea captain's house, in which you can learn all about the lives of seamen, both at work and at home. Also on display are navigational instruments, sailing charts, and ship models.

Penobscot Marine Museum

Portland Museum of Art

Portland Head Lighthouse (Portland) Some people say this is the most photographed lighthouse in the country. It's hard to say if that's true, but having been built in 1791, it's certainly one of the oldest.

Portland Museum of Art (Portland) Lots of works by artists with Maine connections, including Winslow Homer and Andrew Wyeth, are exhibited at Maine's largest art museum.

Blaine House (Augusta) Today the governor lives in this beautiful twenty-eight-room mansion, but when it was built in the 1830s, it was the home of a retired sea captain.

Musical Wonder House (Wiscasset) This grand mansion, built in 1852, is filled with antique music boxes, player pianos, Victrolas, and other musical machines.

Maine Lighthouse (Rockland) You can see the nation's largest collection of lighthouse artifacts at this unusual museum.

Isle au Haut Rocky cliffs, dense forests, and pounding waves greet hikers on this small island.

Acadia National Park (Mount Desert Island) This is one of the nation's most popular national parks, and with its dramatic mountains, rocky coasts, and magnificent vistas, it's easy to see why. Folks come from all over to hike, bike, canoe, sea kayak, rock climb, or just enjoy the incredible scenery.

Great Wass Preserve (Beals Island) Hikers will pass through bogs, forests, and coasts in this magical and often misty spot.

Allagash Wilderness Waterway (Allagash) Remote and spectacular, this is considered the best canoe trip in Maine.

Patten Lumbermen's Museum (Patten) You'll learn all about the lumberman's life at this site, which includes a rebuilt logging camp from the early 1800s, old machinery, and fantastic old photos of lumbermen.

Allagash Wilderness Waterway

Baxter State Park (Millinocket) Visitors flock to this park to climb Mount Katahdin, the highest peak in the state. But those who want to get away from the crowds will have no trouble finding peaceful places to hike and canoe and perhaps even spy a moose.

Washburn-Norlands Living History Center (Livermore) Few places deserve the title "living history center" as much as this spot, where visitors are sent back into the nineteenth century. Those who spend the weekend help out on the farm, cook in the old-fashioned way, and even attend class in the tiny one-room schoolhouse.

FUN FACTS

Maine produces more toothpicks than any other state.

Sir William Phips, who was born in 1650 near Woolwich, became the first British knight born in America. He was knighted by King James II of England for finding a sunken treasure in the Bahamas.

Norway pines, which were once considered the best trees to use as the masts of ships, were not named for the country but for Norway, Maine. Lots of these magnificent trees grew near the town.

Find Out More

There's a lot more to learn about Maine. You might start by checking your local library or bookstore for these titles.

GENERAL STATE HISTORY BOOKS

Pollitt, Fran. *Historic Photos of Maine*. Nashville, TN: Turner Publishing Company, 2008.

Rolde, Neil. *Maine: Downeast and Different: An Illustrated History*. Sun Valley, CA: American Historical Press, 2006.

Talbot, Gerald E. *Maine's Visible Black History: The First Chronicle of Its People*. Gardiner, ME: Tilbury House Publishers, 2006.

OTHER INTERESTING BOOKS

Donnelly, Sara and Meredith Goad. *Insiders' Guide to Portland, Maine*. Guilford, CT: Insider's Guide, 2007.

McNair, Wesley. *Place Called Maine: 24 Writers on the Maine Experience*. Rockport, ME: Down East Books, 2008.

WEBSITES

Native-American Tribes of Maine

www.native-languages.org/maine.htm

Histories, links to reservations, and other information about the American-Indian tribes of Maine can be explored at this website.

Office of Maine Tourism

www.visitmaine.com

The Maine Office of Tourism provides information on sites to see, places to go, weather, and cultural events.

Official Website of the State of Maine

www.state.me.us

Information about Maine's government can be found here. There are details about the state, the governor, the bills that have been recently passed, and other fun facts about the state.

Project Puffin

www.projectpuffin.org

Check on the progress of puffin conservation at this website.

Index

Page numbers in **boldface** are illustrations and charts.

ABOUT THE AUTHORS

Margaret Dornfeld lives in Brooklyn, New York, where she works as a writer, editor, and translator. She has spent many happy summer days on Deer Isle, Maine.

Many years ago, when author Joyce Hart was married, she traveled to Maine for her honeymoon. A couple of decades later, so did her son. Visiting Maine had become a family tradition. Now Hart lives on the northwestern tip of the United States, in a rugged coastal town outside Seattle. She is the author of more than thirty books. When she is not writing, she can be found walking through the woods or along the beaches of Puget Sound with her dog, Molly.